Value-Based Leadership

Henrik Pettersson

Value-Based Leadership

© Henrik Pettersson 2025
Publisher: BoD · Books on Demand, Östermalmstorg 1,
114 42 Stockholm, Sweden, bod@bod.se
Printer: Libri Plureos GmbH, Friedensallee 273,
22763 Hamburg, Germany
ISBN: 978-91-8114-776-6

Foreword – The Art of Leading with Values

"To rule the world, start by ruling yourself."
– Lao Tzu

The best leader is not the one who speaks the loudest, but the one who listens the deepest. Not the one who rules with an iron fist, but the one who leads with ease. This book is an invitation to explore what it truly means to be a values-based leader – to combine ancient wisdom with modern leadership theories to create sustainable results and meaningful impact.

Leadership is about creating movement without forcing, achieving without demanding, and being a catalyst for change. But leadership always begins within yourself. If you can't lead yourself, why would anyone else want to follow you? That's why we start with the foundation: self-leadership. From there, we explore how you can support others to grow, build trust, and create strong relationships. Finally, we move on to leading an organization – with vision, clarity, and values as the core of everything you do.

My name is Henrik Pettersson, and my greatest drive is to help leaders discover and develop their inner strength so that they can become both courageous role models and successful change leaders. Since 2004, I have had the privilege of coaching and inspiring individuals and teams, from beginners to seasoned top performers, in areas such as self-leadership, sales, and personal development.

With over 20 years of experience and thousands of conversations behind me, I have gained a deep understanding of the challenges and opportunities leaders face. I have learned that success is not about always having all the answers but about daring to be human, never stopping learning, and constantly holding on to hope – even when the road is at its toughest.

For me, leadership is about creating real change, both within yourself and in your surroundings. It is a journey that requires courage, humility, and belief in what's possible. This journey is not just my work but my passion and my calling.

This book is your map – or perhaps your GPS – for navigating the landscape of leadership. It is divided into three essential parts so that you can take one insight at a time:

1. **Leading Yourself**
   Start with yourself. Strengthen your self-awareness, take responsibility for your choices, and create an inner calm that influences others.
2. **Leading Others**
   Build trust, inspire, and help people grow. Your leadership is at its strongest when you lift others.
3. **Leading the Organization**
   Define a vision that engages the entire organization. Create clarity and a culture of collaboration and success.

This handbook is designed not only to give you new insights but also to anchor them in your daily life. You'll notice that we sometimes return to certain themes and principles. This is no coincidence. It's because everything in leadership is interconnected. Self-leadership, leading others, and leading the organization are like three interconnected circles – they influence and strengthen one another. Repetition is the key to deepening and creating real change.

The truth is that life as a leader is an ecosystem where you reap what you sow. Are you ready to take responsibility for your development and reach your full potential? This book is not just ink on paper – it's your personal action plan. Together, we will create power, clarity, and purpose in your leadership.

So... open the book, open your mind, and open the door to your full potential.

Let's go!

/Henrik

Not Just a Book
– A Handbook for Your Leadership

"Value-Based Leadership" is not just a book; it is your compass and guide to evolving as a leader on every level. It helps you balance rational decisions with emotional insight and provides powerful tools to reflect on how you lead yourself, others, and your organization.

The book is divided into three parts, highlighting the most critical aspects of sustainable and successful leadership:

Part 1: Leading Yourself
- Explore your values and innermost driving forces.
- Live authentically and in alignment with what you are passionate about.
- Cultivate a strong belief in the future and self-leadership.

Part 2: Leading Others
- Inspire and create positive energy around you.
- Master the art of persuasive arguments and exerting positive influence.
- Build an inclusive culture that fosters development and trust.

Part 3: Leading the Organization
- Set clear goals and a defined strategy.
- Act decisively and solution-oriented.
- Prioritize proactively for long-term success and sustainability.

The three parts are built around questions that help you become a more conscious, inspiring, and action-oriented leader. This book is not just about identifying challenges; it is about creating powerful solutions and strengthening your ability to lead with energy, clarity, and focus.

With this map and compass in hand, you are ready to take the first steps toward a more values-based leadership and to create sustainable results – for yourself, your team, and your organization.

Part 1: Leading Yourself – Rock-Solid ground

Introduction

Knowing Yourself – The Key to True Leadership

Lao Tzu said, "He who knows others is wise, but he who knows himself is enlightened." And indeed, it's easy to spend all your time analyzing others – colleagues, customers, competitors, even the neighbor who always parks crooked. But if you don't know yourself, who are you leading? A confused version of yourself, driven by autopilot and coffee?

Knowing yourself isn't just a nice thought to jot down in the margins of a self-help book. It is the cornerstone of values-based leadership. How can you lead others if you don't know what you stand for? If you're unaware of your triggers, your values, or what makes you lose your temper in a Teams meeting?

Self-Awareness – An Essential Tool (and Yes, It's Challenging)

Do you want to achieve strong results while maintaining your integrity? Start by looking in the mirror. True strength is not about always being right or dominating the room. It's about daring to pause and reflect: Why did I react that way? What really matters here? And no, is it truly necessary to win this argument about the PowerPoint theme?

Self-awareness is about having the courage to recognize both your strengths and your weaknesses. For a leader, this is invaluable. Knowing when to stand firm and when to step back requires more than gut instinct – it requires being rooted in your own values.

Overcoming Yourself – The Greatest Victory

Lao Tzu reminds us that the greatest victory is not defeating others but overcoming ourselves. And let's be honest – managing our own emotions and impulses is often a greater challenge than managing others. It's easy to get swept away by stress, deadlines, or the temptation to say, "I'll do it myself; it's faster that way."

But leadership isn't about doing everything yourself. It's about creating an environment where others can succeed. When you learn to overcome your own reactions and instead act with calmness and clarity, you not only become a better leader – you also become a role model for your team.

The Strength in Knowing Your Path

When you know yourself and stay true to your values, you become like a tree with deep roots: stable, flexible, and unshakable. Living and leading with purpose not only creates sustainable results, but it also brings a sense of meaning. And honestly, who wouldn't want leadership that both inspires and gets things done?

So, ask yourself: Are you ready to face yourself? Because if you are, you will also be ready to face the world – and lead it, in your own way.

Table of Contents

Chapter 1: Character, Self-Awareness, and Courage – The Foundation of Self-Leadership

Leading others always begins with leading yourself. Self-leadership is about building a strong character and developing deep self-awareness. As a leader, you must know what you stand for and have the courage to stay true to it, no matter the situation.

Self-Awareness: Your Foundation

Self-awareness means understanding your strengths, weaknesses, triggers, and values. It provides clarity and confidence in your decision-making. As Lao Tzu says, "He who knows others is wise, but he who knows himself is enlightened."

Building Strong Character

Character is about being reliable and acting with integrity. Nelson Mandela put it well: "I am the master of my fate, the captain of my soul." As a leader, you must build a solid foundation by living in alignment with your values, regardless of circumstances.

Courage: Acting Despite Fear

Courage is about making decisions even when they are uncomfortable. It's about standing firm in your beliefs and handling opposition with integrity. Stories such as Ernest Shackleton's expeditions and Greta Thunberg's unwavering campaign show that courage is not the absence of fear but the ability to act despite it.

Chapter 2: Mental and Physical Strength – Your Inner Engine

Leading yourself requires both mental and physical strength. Mental strength helps you navigate challenges, while physical strength gives you endurance.

Mental Strength: Training Your Mind

Mental strength involves managing pressure and uncertainty. It means prioritizing what truly matters, creating routines to maintain focus, and using tools like breathing techniques and visualization.

Physical Strength: A Strong Body Supports a Strong Mind

Physical health is key to mental clarity. Regular exercise, good sleep, and a balanced diet not only benefit your body – they help you manage stress and maintain energy.

Building Strengthening Habits

Small, consistent actions are the path to endurance. This could be as simple as a daily walk, a gratitude exercise, or prioritizing time for reflection.

Chapter 3: Change and Adaptability – Growing Through Adversity

Change is a constant in life, and your ability to handle it determines your success as a leader.

Navigating the Four Phases of Change

1. Correction: Realizing change is necessary.
2. Chaos: The phase where resistance is at its peak.
3. Confusion: The light at the end of the tunnel begins to appear.
4. Comfort: The new becomes the norm.

Driving Change

As a leader, you must be the catalyst for change and help your team see the long-term benefits.

Inspiration from Role Models

Examples such as Malala Yousafzai and Greta Thunberg show that the courage to stay true to your values is the foundation for leading through change.

Chapter 4: Values and Self-Discipline – Leading Yourself with Integrity

Values are your moral compass. Self-discipline is the tool that helps you live in alignment with them.

Living Your Values

Values are not just words – they are actions. Leaders like Nelson Mandela and Alexander the Great demonstrated that living your values builds trust.

Self-Discipline: The Key to Real Success

Self-discipline is about doing what is necessary, not what is convenient. It is the small, daily choices that lead to greater results.

Practical Tools

- Planning: Set clear goals and prioritize.
- Action: Act consistently, even when it's tough.
- Reflection: Evaluate and adjust.

Chapter 5: Stress Management and Balance – From Enemy to Superpower

Stress is not your enemy – how you handle it makes all the difference.

Transforming Stress into an Asset

Short-term stress can sharpen your focus and boost your performance. The key is to prevent stress from becoming chronic.

Practical Strategies

- Breathing Control: Use techniques like box-breathing.
- Self-Talk: Replace negative thoughts with positive affirmations.
- Visualization: Train your mind to see success.

Building Long-Term Stress Resilience

- Prioritize sleep, nutrition, and exercise.
- Set boundaries and learn to say no.
- Focus on what you can control.

How to Maintain High Energy Levels – The Demands You Must Place on Yourself

No one is going to hold your hand here.
No one is going to knock on your door and say:
"Excuse me, but are you managing your sleep? Are you getting proper nutrition? Are you pushing the boundaries of your thinking?"
If you don't do it yourself – you'll fall. And when you fall, you take those who look up to you down with you. Leadership always starts with yourself. Here are the uncomfortable truths and demands you must have the courage to place – on yourself:

1. Sleep – Your Secret Superpower
Fatigue is not a badge of honor. No one thanks you for working around the clock with a brain running on fumes. Want to be sharp, focused, and at the top of your game? Sleep. It's simple. Do it.

2. Nutrition – Fuel for Your Brain and Body
Living on coffee and whatever happens to be in the vending machine? Convenient, maybe, but it won't keep you alive – or in a leadership role. Food is fuel, not filler. Choose what you eat as if your leadership depended on it. Because it does.

3. Exercise – It's Not About Beach 2025
It's about endurance. Enduring late nights when needed, staying mentally present when it gets tough. Strong body, strong mind. Period.

4. Knowledge – Never Stay in Your Comfort Zone
Read. Learn. Replenish. Grow or wither – that's the choice. The question is: do you want to stay ahead or be overtaken?

5. Self-Leadership – No One Else Will Prioritize You
It's painful but true. If you don't put yourself first – your needs, your growth, your time – how can you lead others?
Self-leadership isn't selfish. It's essential.

The Core of Leadership: Demands Define Quality

Want to know how good you are as a leader?
Look at the standards you set for yourself – and whether you
have the discipline to meet them. Every. Day.
Are your demands high enough?
Or are you coasting on past achievements?
Leadership isn't just a title.
It's the sum of everything you do, every single day. So I ask you:
Are you ready to set the demands it takes – and truly lead?

Chapter 1

Character, Self-Awareness, and Courage

Stability or Chaos – Rock-solid ground or Sand?

Let's talk about nuclear power. In the nucleus of an atom, two forces work together: the electromagnetic force and the strong nuclear force. When the core is stable, balance is created along with a powerful lifting capacity. But if the core falters? Everything falls apart.

The exact same principle applies to people, teams, and organizations. When the inside – the culture, values, identity – is solid, no external storm can shake it. But if you build on sand, you can be sure that the first gust of wind will topple the entire structure.

Too many organizations focus all their energy on the surface: flashy campaigns, sleek PowerPoints, and polished facades. But if you don't have a stable core – what happens when the storm hits? Exactly. A sandstorm.

Do you want to build on Rock-solid ground? Then start from within.

Scouting for Strong Characters – What Are You Made Of?

Nelson Mandela. Not just a freedom fighter – a living testament to unwavering character.

27 years on Robben Island. 27 years where his body was imprisoned, but his mind was free. On the wall of his cell, he had a quote:
"I am the master of my fate, and the captain of my soul."
That attitude. That inner strength. That is what creates real leaders.

So, what distinguishes a strong character from a weak one?

In my experience, it boils down to three things:

- **Endurance:** When others falter, you hold the line. Five years from now, today's challenges will be mere training sessions.
- **Courage:** You listen to your inner compass, not to what everyone else thinks.
- **Action:** You don't just talk – you act.

Strong Character Is Built on Clear Principles

It's not about appearances, titles, or that perfect LinkedIn feed. Strong character is the backbone. Here are three pairs of traits you need to master:

- **Honesty & Reliability:** Stop lying, even to yourself. Own the truth, even when it stings.
- **Integrity & Confidence:** Do what you say you will do. Always.
- **Endurance & Discipline:** Small steps. Every day. No one sees them – but the results speak for themselves.

Do You Want to Build a Strong Character?

Here are the questions you need to ask yourself:

- Who am I – really?
- What values do I live by, even when no one is watching?
- What motivates me?
- What makes me proud?
- What traits do I want others to associate with me?

The questions are uncomfortable. But they are necessary. Because without digging into them – how can you build something that lasts?

Seven Principles That Define Strong Characters:

1. **They live by principles**. They don't waver just because of headwinds.
2. **They build standards** – not facades. Surface can impress. But character endures.
3. **They keep their promises**. Always. Words = actions.
4. **They are constantly learning**. No complacency. Just hunger for growth.
5. **They have a strategy** – not just tactics. Quick wins are fun, but they think long-term.
6. **They never give up**. Challenges? Bring it on.
7. **They build confidence through action**. Confidence isn't given. It's built – step by step.

So, What Will You Do?

Are you building your leadership on sand or Rock-solid ground?
Do you want to be a leader that others genuinely respect?
Then it's time to stop talking and start acting.

Start by:

1. Defining your values.
2. Standing by them – no matter what.
3. Stopping the chase for validation – and building results.

The **Character Matrix** is about building from within. Becoming a leader who stands firm. One who doesn't just survive the storm – but can lead others through it.

So, who are you – really?

And what are you doing today to shape your inner strength?
  (See the appendix at the end of the chapter for detailed guidance and opportunities to create your own leadership matrix that fits YOU.)

Courage and Overcoming Fears
COURAGE – The True Superpower in Leadership

"Anxiety, rule-following, and an overdose of meetings – stifle leaders' initiative. Doing things the right way has become more important than doing the right things."

Striking, isn't it? Patrik Hall, professor of political science, hits the nail on the head. When administration and micromanagement take over, leadership becomes a pale shadow of what it should be: a force for change, inspiration, and progress.

Courage isn't a fluffy word for visionaries – it's the fuel that separates real leaders from bureaucratic paper tigers. It's not about going with the flow but standing firm in the storm when others retreat. And it's not just about handling daily challenges – it's about drawing strength from your values and leading through them.

The Story of Shackleton – A Leadership Icon

Few stories demonstrate courage in leadership as powerfully as Ernest Shackleton's Antarctic expedition.

The year was 1914, and Shackleton planned to become the first to cross the frozen continent on foot. But the plan took a dramatic turn when the ship **Endurance** became trapped in ice and eventually sank. He and his crew faced a seemingly impossible challenge: surviving in one of the world's most inhospitable environments.

What made Shackleton such an incredible leader was his ability to never lose sight of what truly mattered – keeping his team alive and inspiring them to never give up. By building trust and setting clear goals, he became a beacon of hope for his men.

For months, they trekked across ice fields and braved perilous seas. Shackleton shared resources equally, always prioritized his crew's well-being, and demonstrated that leadership in its purest form is about acting on your values – no matter the circumstances. Ultimately, he succeeded in bringing all his men home without a single loss.

Shackleton's journey reminds us that courage is more than physical strength – it is a moral force to stand by your principles and lead with heart and vision, even in the darkest moments.

Courage – The Key to Overcoming Fear

2025. Donald Trump steps back into the White House for his second term, and the nation finds itself in a whirlwind of change. In just a few days, old structures are overturned, and new, controversial decisions set the tone for what lies ahead. What do we, as leaders, do when the storm rages around us? Here's the answer: We step forward. We show courage. And we hold on to our character.

For it is precisely in such moments—when values are tested, and pressure mounts—that we reveal who we truly are. Leading with value-based leadership isn't about going with the flow or hiding behind convenient excuses. It's about daring to stand up, daring to say, "This is what I believe in, and this is what's right."

The beginning of 2025 taught us something important once again: Leadership isn't defined when it's easy—it's defined when it's hard. Courage isn't the absence of fear; it's acting in spite of it. Character is choosing the right path, even when the easier path beckons. And value-based leadership is about building your compass around integrity, courage, and long-term purpose—regardless of external pressures.

As Bishop Mariann Edgar Budde expressed it: "**We must have the courage to stand up for what we know is right.**" That's a challenge for all of us. So, the question is: What do you stand for? When the pressure mounts and the choices feel heavy—will you lead with integrity, or will you waver?

Value-based leadership begins with you. It's your character that shapes the world you leave behind. Now is the time to act. Every day, every decision—let courage be your compass and your values your guiding light. Because it is through action that we create true change.

Courage also means daring to **face yourself and your fears**. Leading yourself is a journey where you challenge yourself to see your limitations but also to accept your humanity. How can we create a solid foundation of courage in our lives? The answer lies in continuously building small acts of integrity and strength, every day.

This journey is not linear. But it is in the willingness to keep moving forward, no matter the obstacles, that we find our strength. So, no matter what challenges you face, remember: The courage to act on your values is always the path to true leadership.

Courage in Leadership Means:

- Breaking through pointless rules and sluggish processes.
- Prioritizing results over playing it safe.
- Skipping meetings where "no one really knows why we're here."
- Resisting the call for more resources in already overloaded organizations.
- Daring to make decisions when uncertainty is at its peak.

Courage requires risk. Without risk? No courage is needed. And if you always choose comfort, why even call yourself a leader?

Questions for Braver Leadership:

- How can we deliver MORE value with fewer resources?
- How can we reduce bureaucracy without losing quality?
- How do we ensure meetings actually lead somewhere?
- What tough conversations have you postponed in the past month?
- What would you do differently today if you weren't afraid of failure?

Nine Types of Courage You Need as a Leader:

1. **Moral Courage – Standing Firm in the Storm**
   83% of 800 leaders highlighted this as the most important trait. Speaking up for what's right – even when it's uncomfortable. Courage means standing for the right things – even when it costs you. Silence is often the greatest betrayal.

2. **Courage and Performance – Daring to Start Despite Uncertainty**
   Jessica Diggins, world champion cross-country skier, said after her toughest battle with an eating disorder: "Even having the courage to stand at the starting line is a victory in itself."

3. **Courage to Face Challenges – Painting Yourself into a Corner**
   As JFK said: "We choose to go to the moon in this decade and do the other things, not because they are easy, but because they are hard."

4. **Courage to Remain Loyal – Staying True Without Wavering**
   Loyalty isn't blind obedience. It's standing firm with your values, your team, and the people you've promised to support – even when it's tough.

5. **Courage to Take Your Own Path**
   George Bernard Shaw said it best: "The reasonable man adapts himself to the world. The unreasonable one persists in trying to adapt the world to himself."

6. **Courage to Let Go of Control**
   Steve Jobs knew what he was talking about: "We hire smart people to tell us what to do."

7. **Courage to Show Vulnerability – True Confidence**
   Daring to say: "I don't know." „I was wrong." „I need help."

8. **Courage to Have the Tough Conversations**
   Ranked as one of the most important leadership traits. Courage is saying what needs to be said – without sugarcoating it.

17. **Courage to Set Demanding Standards – Holding High Expectations**
    Saying: "We can do better." „This isn't enough." „We expect more."

Courage Isn't Just a Word – It's Your Responsibility as a Leader

Courage is standing up. Courage is taking action, even when it's difficult. Courage is being the one who lifts others, not just yourself.

So, what are you waiting for? Leadership isn't a popularity contest. It's about doing what's right.

Chapter 2

Mental and Physical Strength – Your Inner Engine

It was an autumn day in Helsingborg. I had landed for an assignment to "boost" corporate cultures. The flight was smooth, and the weather was nice. I stepped off the plane, laptop bag over my shoulder, ready for the pre-booked taxi.

No taxi. No sign with my name. Just me and my growing irritation.

A few phone calls later, frustration at its peak, and some deep breaths: My booking had been canceled. "Can I just grab a free taxi here?" I suggested. The answer? "That won't work."

Stress was boiling over. But my assignment awaited. Time to get it together.

Breathe. Calmly. Focus.

It worked out. The workshop? Magical. But that moment, when I was millimeters away from losing it, reminded me once again of a vital truth:

Mental strength is tested all the time.

Lessons for Those Who Want to Lead with Power:
- You've heard it a thousand times, but it doesn't matter – this one must be repeated until it sinks in: You can't control everything around you. But **you can control yourself.**
- Freaking out solves nothing – it only drains energy.
- **Mental leadership** = maintaining focus even when it's stormy.

How often have you let irritation drain your energy?

Here's How You Build Mental Strength:

- Own your reaction.
- Practice staying calm under pressure.
- Lead yourself instead of letting the chaos lead you.

Want to sharpen your mental edge? Start with your breathing. Start with your thoughts. Start with yourself.

Mental Effectiveness – Leading Yourself with Power

John F. Kennedy said it best:

"We choose to go to the moon, not because it is easy, but because it is hard."
    Thank you, JFK – spot on. True strength is born from resistance. Astronauts, elite athletes – and you as a leader. It's time to master your inner self.

Mental effectiveness = using your energy wisely. Like an engine – the cleaner the fuel, the more power.

Skip the mental chatter. Feed yourself with what works. An athlete creates routines to perform when it matters – why shouldn't you?

What Builds Mental Strength:

1. **Knowledge & Competence:** The more you know, the less likely you are to lose control.

2. **Physical Health:** Your engine. Exercise = sharpness & endurance. Good food = clearer thinking.

3. **Self-Confidence & Body Language:** Stand tall. Look people in the eye. „Fake it" until you „make it."

4. **Prioritization:** Know the difference between urgent and important.

5. **Discipline:** Motivation doesn't last – it's like showering, which is why it's recommended daily. Do the work anyway.

What Drains You:

- **Negative Thought Patterns:** Less complaining, more action.
- **Anger & Revenge:** Satisfying in the moment, draining in the long run.
- **Energy Thieves:** Cut out negativity.
- **Meaningless Conflicts:** Focus on what you can control.

And most importantly: **Think bigger. Act bigger. Dare more.**

Not because it's easy – but because it's hard.

SELF-CONFIDENCE – HOW TO TRULY ACHIEVE IT

Self-confidence. It's like the Holy Grail of personal development – mythical, sought after, and hard to find. But here's the truth: self-confidence isn't something you're born with. It's not reserved for charismatic stars on stage. No, it's a trait you build. From the ground up.

And perhaps no story illustrates this better than the journey of Oprah Winfrey. Oprah, now one of the most successful women in the world, began her life in poverty under challenging circumstances. She faced discrimination, endured abuse, and received harsh criticism at the start of her career. But by refusing to let her past define her and by building her self-confidence brick by brick – through small victories and grand visions – she became an icon for millions.

Oprah is living proof that self-confidence is something we create – not something we are given.

So, how do you build that unwavering sense of being able to handle life's challenges, no matter what? Here are seven brutally honest keys to true, strong self-confidence:

1. **Optimism – Stop Blaming the Weather**
   A true winner sees opportunities where others see problems.
- Problems = Potential for growth.
- Changes = New chances.

27

- Challenges = Free personal development.

Does this sound overly peppy? Sure, but the truth is simple: self-confidence depends on where you direct your focus. Are you stuck complaining about things you can't control? Or are you channeling your energy into what you can influence? Stop being a passenger in your own life.

2. Adaptability – Flexibility Is Not Weakness

Charles Darwin said: "It is not the strongest who survive, but those most adaptable to change."

Lesson: If you refuse to change because it's "uncomfortable," someone else will overtake you. The world is changing – you can either evolve or become a fossil. Self-confidence is born from agility. Dare to try new things. Adjust. Adapt. Grow.

3. Grit – The Ability to Never Give Up (Even When It Hurts)

Grit, coined by psychologist Angela Duckworth, isn't a trendy hashtag. It's the essence of perseverance.

It's not about IQ or talent. It's about:
- Enduring the last 20% when others give up.
- Pushing forward even when it sucks.
- Taking one more step – even when motivation has vanished.

Winners never quit. Quitters never win. So, how far are you willing to go to achieve your goal?

4. See Opportunities Over Obstacles – Stop Complaining, Start SOLVING

When golf star Linn Grant was asked how she handles the pressure of every putt being worth money, she responded: "What do you mean? It's incredibly motivating!"

Exactly. What scares some motivates others. Want strong self-confidence? Learn to see opportunities where others see risks.
- Problem? Exciting challenge.
- Pressure? Adrenaline for growth.
- Setback? Lesson.

Time to stop whining. Time to start acting.

5. **Belief in Success – Fake It till You Make It? No, BELIEVE It Till You BECOME It**

   Olympic gold medalist Nils van der Poel was asked: "Will you win gold?" His answer? „I'd be very surprised if I didn't."

This isn't arrogance. It's mental programming. If you don't believe you can win, why should anyone else?

   Visualize success. See it. Feel it. Act as though it's already yours.

6. **Physical Habits – The Body Fuels Confidence**

   Let's be honest – you can't think your way to confidence if your body is struggling.

A. **Eat for strength**
- **Drink enough water**: Hydration is key to energy and focus. Aim for at least 1.5-2 liters a day.
- **Prioritize fresh produce**: Aim to eat more fresh, unprocessed foods.
- **Avoid excessive caffeine intake**: Too much coffee can increase stress and reduce sleep quality.
- **Reduce fast carbohydrates**. Increase protein intake.

B. **Exercise for energy**
- Movement produces dopamine. Dopamine = confidence.
- Find a pace that suits YOU where you are right now, and that you can keep for the rest of the year.
- **Vary the exercise:** Combine fitness (eg cycling or running) with strength and mobility to avoid boredom.
- **Plan active recovery:** Days of yoga, walking or light exercise help the body recover.

C. **Posture – The direct boost method**
- **Focus on breathing:** Deep breathing can reduce stress and increase oxygenation in the body.
- Use your hands consciously: Gestures strengthen your message and give more energy to your communication.

- **Avoid hunched-over posture:** Add a reminder to sit or stand straight even when you're tired.
- Maintain eye contact.
- Stretch yourself.

"What can I adjust today to take ONE step towards better energy and confidence?"

7. Acknowledgment – Small Wins Build a Big Winning Mentality

Confidence is born from evidence. Small wins lead to big results. By creating momentum with small interim goals, you strengthen the belief in yourself and your abilities.

How to build momentum:

- Did you manage 20 push-ups? Celebrate it.
- Did you give a presentation without trembling? Nice!
- Did you take the first step towards a new project? Great job!
- Did you learn something new today? Fantastic – give yourself a round of applause!
- Did you say no to something that wasn't important? Good prioritization – you are on the right track!

Why Small Wins Matter:

Small successes are the fuel for big dreams. The positive feelings from achieving intermediate goals strengthen your belief that you can also achieve bigger goals. It's about creating a positive spiral where self-confidence breeds action and action breeds more self-confidence.

Make it concrete:

- Write down your wins: Take two minutes every evening and write down three small things you did well during the day. This habit will help you notice successes and strengthen your mental strength.

- Visualize the successes: Create a progress board or use an app to see how your small wins lead towards your main goal.

Remember:

- Self-confidence grows from continuity – small steps every day lead to big results.
- Small wins create momentum, and momentum is the key to keeping energy and motivation up.

"Small successes are the little sparks that light the fire of big dreams."

Summary – Self-Confidence Is Your Choice

Self-confidence isn't something you wish for. It's something you create.
　Want it? Then you must:
- Act despite fear.
- See opportunities where others see problems.
- Do the work – even when no one is watching.

So, what are you waiting for? Start today. Small steps. Build your strength. And become the best version of yourself.

Formulärets nederkant

Chapter 3

The Art of Handling Change – For Those Who Want to Stop Hiding Behind Excuses

"Progress is impossible without change, and those who cannot change their minds cannot change anything."

"Progress is impossible without change, and those who cannot change their minds cannot change anything."

Change. That uncomfortable, unwelcome monster that appears just when you've started feeling a bit too comfortable. Yet it is precisely change that separates those who grow from those who remain stuck. Change IS growth. Change IS progress. And ignoring it? That's like trying to swim with a concrete block tied to your feet.

Niccolò Machiavelli put it bluntly: "There is nothing more difficult to carry out, more perilous to conduct, or more uncertain in its success than to introduce new ideas. Innovation meets resistance from those who have benefited from old systems – and only weak support from those who may benefit from the new."

Read that again. There lies the problem. Being the first to embrace change means enduring criticism, skepticism, and a fair amount of passive resistance.

And yet, it is precisely those who dare to change that make history.

A recent example is the story of Greta Thunberg. When she was 15 years old, sitting outside Sweden's parliament with a handwritten sign demanding climate action, no one could have predicted that this simple act would spark a global movement. Greta faced criticism, ridicule, and resistance from powerful figures – but she stood firm in her principles. Through her determination and courage, she has inspired millions of young people to engage in climate activism and shown that even a single voice can create a wave of change.

Greta's journey demonstrates that change isn't about having power or resources. It's about daring to take the first step and believing in your ability to make a difference. Her story is a reminder that we all have the potential to impact the world around us – if only we dare.

So, the next time the monster of change shows up, dare to ask yourself: What would Greta do? The answer might not make the journey easier, but it will make it more meaningful.

The Four Phases of Change – Welcome to the 4*C Model

Change is rarely a simple journey from point A to B. It's more like a roller coaster where you're sometimes upside down, wondering why you even embarked on this ride.

Decision Point

Here are the four phases you and your team will go through:

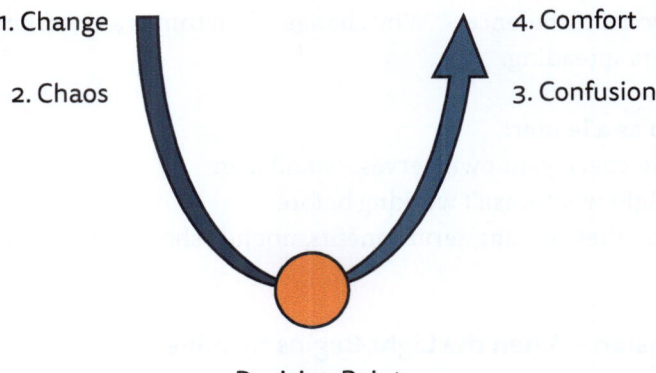

1. Change

2. Chaos

4. Comfort

3. Confusion

Decision Point

1. Change – When the Transformation Begins

Congratulations! You've realized that something needs to change. But everyone else? They're not as excited.

Common reactions:
- Silent skepticism.
- "But we've always done it this way..."
- Searching for comfort in old patterns.

Your job as a leader:
- Be extremely clear about why the change is necessary.
- Communicate three concrete benefits of the change.
- Acknowledge concerns – but don't leave room for excuses.

2. Chaos – When Resistance Peaks

Welcome to the temple of doubt. Confusion, frustration, and a chorus of voices whispering:
"This will never work."

Common reactions:
- Questioning the decision.
- Emotional turbulence – "Why change when things are working?"
- Rumors spreading.

Your job as a leader:
- Double-check your own nerves – stand firm.
- Highlight what wasn't working before.
- Remind them of long-term benefits, not just short-term pains.

3. Confusion – When the Light Begins to Shine

Suddenly, people start realizing that the new way might... actually work? But confusion still lingers.

Common reactions:
- Small wins become noticeable.

- Curiosity grows – but skeptics remain.
- Someone dares to say, "Hmm... maybe it's not so bad after all."

Your job as a leader:
- Encourage small victories – big time.
- Highlight positive changes.
- Share short-term wins and connect them to long-term goals.

4. Comfort – When the New Becomes Normal

Ah, finally! Change is no longer "change" – it's the new standard.

Common reactions:
- Stability is restored.
- New routines feel natural.
- Team confidence increases.

Your job as a leader:
- Celebrate those who made the journey possible.
- Remind the team of the journey – and what they've overcome.
- Start planning the next level of development.

The Key: Stop Waiting – Start the Change NOW!

Change without action is like standing in front of a fireplace and asking for warmth without lighting a match.
Initiative is born from three factors:

- **Intention:** You must want something.
- **Inspiration:** You must see a possible future.
- **Initiative:** You must act – even if it feels uncomfortable.

So, Are You Ready to Truly Handle Change?

Here's the truth:

- Change is not a threat – it's your best friend.
- Your attitude determines whether you succeed or get stuck.
- Possible or impossible? It's **always your choice**.

So, what's the next change you need to embrace?

And most importantly: **When are you going to start**?

The Art of Letting Go – For a Life with More Energy and Focus

"And so, it is important to be able to let go."
These were the closing words of an old abbot's evening prayer. The next day, a young, frustrated monk approached him and asked: "How do you let go of failures, disappointments, and broken hearts when bitterness suffocates positive thoughts?"
The abbot smiled, invited him for tea, and handed him a cup. He began pouring boiling water into it. The cup grew hotter and hotter until the pain became too much – the monk let go of the cup, which shattered on the floor. „You see... it wasn't so hard to let go."

Why Is It So Hard to Let Go?

We know we should. We understand it would do us good. And yet, we hold on. Why?
- **Grief and betrayal:** We think we need to remember in order to learn.
- **Failures and shame:** Letting go feels like admitting defeat.
- **Bitterness and disappointment:** We get stuck in "it shouldn't have happened."
- **Fear of losing control:** Holding on feels safe – even if it drags us down.

But the truth? What really holds us back is the fear of moving forward.

An example of the power of letting go is the story of Simone Biles, the multiple Olympic gold medalist in gymnastics. During the Tokyo 2021 Olympics, she chose to withdraw from several events, even though she was the favorite to win. She faced a storm of criticism and global expectations. But Simone realized that her mental health and well-being were more important than medals.

By letting go of the pressure to perform and external demands, she demonstrated incredible courage and set a new example of what true success is about. Simone showed that sometimes the most powerful thing we can do is step back, reflect, and dare to prioritize ourselves.

Her decision inspired many to rethink their own views on achievement and balance in life. Simone Biles reminds us that letting go is not a sign of weakness – it is an act of strength and self-respect.

The Three Circles of Control and Influence

To let go, you first need to understand what you're holding on to. The American author Byron Katie divided this into three circles of control ("or business model"):

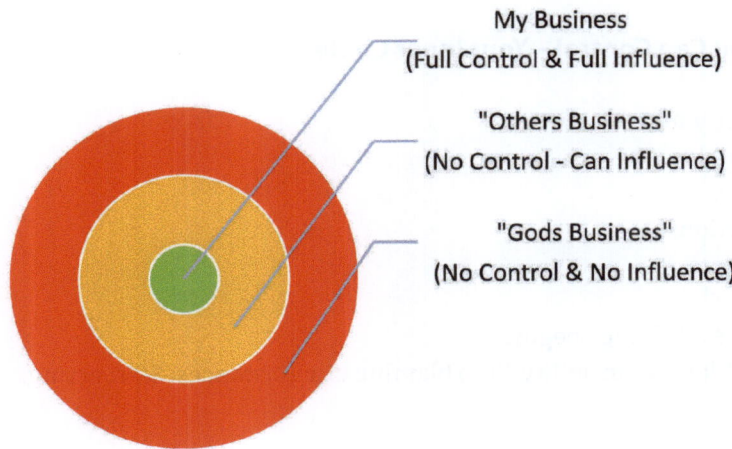

My Business
(Full Control & Full Influence)

"Others Business"
(No Control - Can Influence)

"Gods Business"
(No Control & No Influence)

1. Things You Cannot Control or Influence

Examples:
- The weather.
- Economic crises.
- Other people's opinions.
- Inflation.
- Global conflicts.

If you can't influence it – why waste energy on it?
Solution: Let go. Stop dwelling. Focus on what you can influence.

2. Other People's Behaviors (No Control but Can Influence)

Examples:
- Your children's choices.
- Colleagues' performances.
- Your partner's opinions.

You have influence, but not total control.
Solution: Be a role model. Inspire through action, refine your argumentation, but never force.

3. What You Can Control – Your Inner Circle

This is where your real power lies:
- Your thoughts.
- Your focus.
- Your reactions.
- Your choices.

This is where all change begins.
Solution: Take responsibility. Stop blaming circumstances. Start acting.

How to Let Go in Practice:

1. **Identify what you're holding on to.**
   What's nagging at you? What are you dwelling on? Write it down. Seeing it on paper lessens its power.
2. **Ask yourself: Can I influence this?**
   Is it something within your control? If not – let it go.
3. **Shift your focus.**
   Redirect your energy toward what you can actually change.
4. **Visualize the relief.**
   How would it feel to simply let go? Peace. Clarity. Calm.
5. **Take action.**
   Letting go isn't just about mindset. It's about action:
- Apologize.
- Finish old projects.
- Cut ties with negative relationships.

But What If I Can't Let Go?

Yes, you can. But let's be honest:
- Holding on feels safe and comfortable.
- Dwelling can sometimes feel like a shield.
- Letting go means taking a step forward – and that requires courage.

But the truth is simple:
You can't accept something new if your hands are still holding on to the old.

Buddha's Four Truths:

1. Life contains suffering.
2. The root of suffering is attachment.
3. There is a way out of suffering.
4. The way is to let go of emotional attachments.

Emotional Attachments – Do You Dare to Let Go and Grow as a Leader?

Emotional attachments are not just things or relationships – they can also be ways of working, thought patterns, and old routines that we cling to. It could be the heirloom jewelry that sits in a drawer or a method at work that was once brilliant but now feels outdated. Why do we hold on to them? Because they once meant something. Because they feel safe. And because letting go can be both scary and uncomfortable.

But here's the question you need to ask yourself: Does this still serve me, or is it holding me back?

As a leader, it's easy to get stuck in "this is how we've always done it." It could be a process, a way of working, or even an idea about your own role that is slowing you and your team down. It feels safe, but safety isn't where growth happens. Being a values-driven leader means daring to challenge yourself and your way of thinking. It means being brave enough not only to look at what's working but also to acknowledge what has stagnated.

Here's a challenge for you: Identify an area in your life or leadership where you're holding onto something that no longer feels right. It could be an old habit, a routine, or even a relationship. Hold it up in front of you and ask: Does this give me and my team strength, or is it just something I'm carrying out of habit?

When you dare to let go of what no longer lifts you, you create space – not just in your home or your heart but also in your organization. Space for the new, for what drives development, and for what aligns with your values.

Letting go isn't about losing something. It's about consciously choosing what deserves to come along on the journey forward – and daring to create something better. So, do you dare to take the step?

The Results When You Let Go:

- Freed energy. Less stress. More clarity.
- Better focus. You can finally put energy into what truly matters.
- Stronger leadership. When you let go of the unimportant, you lead with power.

So, What Are You Holding Onto Right Now?

And most importantly:
Are you ready to let go – or will you hold on until it burns?

Chapter 4

Values and Self-Discipline – What You Do When No One Is Watching

Let's talk about self-leadership. Not the fluffy "personal development" that sounds good in theory but no one actually follows. I'm talking about real self-leadership – the kind that shapes strong leaders and earns respect, not through words, but through actions.

Extraordinary Self-Leadership – A Lesson from Alexander the Great

In 325 BCE, during the Persian campaign, Alexander the Great marched his army through the relentless Gedrosian Desert. Thirst, heat, and exhaustion pushed his soldiers to their breaking point. One soldier approached Alexander with a helmet filled with water – a symbol of survival.

What did Alexander do? He took the helmet, raised it to the sun, and poured the water slowly into the sand in front of his exhausted troops. His message?

"Too much for one, too little for so many."

Through this action, he demonstrated that he would never demand anything from his soldiers that he wasn't willing to endure himself. That is self-leadership. That is leading with backbone – not just words.

Want to Build Strong Self-Leadership? Here Are the Principles:

1. Positive Thinking – Stop Complaining, Start Solving
Strong self-leadership begins with how you view the world:
- See solutions, not problems.
- Learn from setbacks instead of getting stuck in them.
- Replace "Why is this happening to me?" with "What can I learn from this?"

Positive thinking isn't naïve. It's strategic. Nelson Mandela, who spent 27 years in prison without losing his vision of freedom, is proof of this. His mindset showed that a positive outlook can drive change – both within ourselves and in the world around us.

Story: The Optimistic Farmer

Once, there was a farmer who always responded with, "It could have been worse." When his fields were destroyed by a storm, he said, "It could have been worse – I still have my home." When his only cow died, he said, "It could have been worse – I still have my family." His attitude spread, and soon the entire village began thinking the same way. Even when everything seems hopeless, there is always a way forward if you choose to see it.

2. Courage and Perseverance – Dare to Stand Firm in the Storm
Courage isn't about being fearless. It's about acting despite fear:
- Dare to make tough decisions.
- Rise when you fall.
- Hold the line – even when it costs you.

Courage is the trait that transforms challenges into strength. Think of Malala Yousafzai, who, despite threats from the Taliban, continued to fight for girls' right to education. Her courage inspires millions.

3. Turning Weakness into Strength – Own Your Failures
Failures aren't your end. They're your education:
- J.K. Rowling was rejected by 12 publishers before Harry Potter became a global success.
- Michael Jordan was cut from his first basketball team.

It's not how you fall that matters – it's how long you stay down before you get back up.

Sara Blakely and Spanx

Sara Blakely, the founder of Spanx, started her career selling fax machines door-to-door. She faced countless rejections and quickly realized it wasn't a career she wanted to pursue. Instead of letting setbacks define her, she saw each "no" as an opportunity to learn resilience.

One day, she came up with the idea for Spanx when she cut the feet off a pair of pantyhose to get a more flattering look under white pants. The idea was simple, but the road to success was full of challenges. She had no experience in the fashion industry, no business education, and very little startup capital. Despite this, she fought to get her product manufactured and convinced stores to sell it.

Blakely pitched her idea to countless manufacturers, and almost all said no. But she didn't give up. Eventually, she found a factory that believed in her vision. The rest is history. Spanx became a global success, and Sara Blakely became one of the world's youngest self-made billionaires.

Lesson: Sara Blakely shows that failures and rejections aren't obstacles – they're stepping stones on the path to success. It's about daring to try again, being creative, and owning your setbacks as part of the journey.

4. Letting Go of Negative Events – Pack Lighter

Negative experiences are like heavy baggage. How long do you plan to carry it?

- Failures? Learn and move on.
- Bitterness? It only benefits the person you're angry with.
- Fear? It stops you from growing.

Pack Lighter.

You can't change what has happened, but you can decide how much it will affect you. Let go of what no longer serves you – and free yourself to take the next step.

5. Confidence Through Action – Stop Waiting to Feel Ready

Confidence is Not a Gift – It's Something You Build by Taking Action.

- Want to feel confident? Do something.
- Want to feel secure? Take the lead.
- Want to win? Start playing.

Your body language affects how you feel:

- **Stand tall.**

- **Maintain eye contact.**
- **Speak clearly.**

You become what you do – not what you think you should do. Start taking action now. The rest will follow.

6. **Internal Motivation – Your 'Why' Is Your Fuel**

   External praise? Bonuses? Likes on social media? Fun, but they don't last. True motivation must come from within:
   - What drives you?
   - What do you want to leave behind?
   - What are you fighting for?

Find your "why" – and you'll find your strength.

7. **The Ability to Change – Evolve or Stagnate**

   Change is uncomfortable. But you know what's worse? Getting stuck:
   - Charles Darwin said it best: Again – "It is not the strongest who survive, but the ones most adaptable to change."
   - Let go of old patterns that no longer serve you. Want to grow? Dare to change.

Self-Discipline and GRIT – Your Superpower

GRIT – Your Superpower as a Value-Based Leader

GRIT is about raw, uncompromising perseverance and the ability to stick to your values and goals. It's not an innate trait; it's a muscle that must be trained daily. GRIT is like building a house – every brick you lay is an action that strengthens the foundation. It's about showing up, even when you don't feel like it, and seeing every setback as an opportunity to grow.

As a leader, this means:
- **Standing firm when others falter.** When the team doubts or the situation becomes uncertain, you show the way. You're not the one hiding behind convenience or excuses – you're the one stepping into the storm first.

- **Acting in alignment with your values – even when it costs you.** The right choice is often the hardest. Standing up for your principles, even in the face of resistance, is what sets a true leader apart from one who merely follows the crowd. Think of Martin Luther King Jr., who, despite hate and threats, refused to compromise his ideals. He demonstrated that leadership requires courage and consistency.
- **Persisting when the "easier path" is tempting.** GRIT is about letting principles, not convenience, guide your actions. When others choose shortcuts or give up, you keep moving forward. You know that success isn't about always winning but about never giving up.

How to strenghten your GRIT

1. **Develop a habit of facing challenges.** When you encounter problems, ask yourself: What can I learn from this? Start viewing challenges as opportunities to build your perseverance.
2. **Build small victories.** GRIT isn't about winning big battles right away. It's about accumulating small, daily wins. Wake up on time. Keep your promises. Go the extra mile. These actions build your strength over time.
3. **Surround yourself with the right people.** GRIT is contagious. If you surround yourself with people who have perseverance and courage, their attitude will strengthen yours. Ensure your network inspires rather than distracts.
4. **Embrace discomfort.** Success is often boring and repetitive. It's about doing what's required, not what's fun. Want to be the best? Learn to love the monotony.

An Inspiring Example – Mo Farah and the Last Lap

Think of runner Mo Farah, who fell during one of his heats at the 2012 Olympics. While others ran ahead, he got up and started chasing. Not only did he make it to the final – he won the gold. What drives someone to get up when everything seems lost? GRIT.

Mo Farah's story shows that GRIT isn't about perfection. It's about rising every time you fall and never letting a mistake define your journey.

GRIT in Practice for Leaders

One of the most inspiring examples of GRIT comes from Sir Edmund Hillary and Tenzing Norgay, the first people to ever summit Mount Everest on May 29, 1953. It wasn't talent or luck that took them to the top – it was their unwavering determination and the will to keep going despite extreme cold, lack of oxygen, and life-threatening conditions. They knew that success wasn't about a perfect journey but about never stopping.

As a leader, you can learn from their journey:

- **Have a clear vision.** What is your "Everest"? Ensure every step you take moves you closer to the summit.
- **Perseverance beats talent.** It's not the fastest or smartest who win but those who refuse to give up.
- **Work together.** No one climbs a mountain alone. The support from Tenzing Norgay was crucial to Hillary's success.

Your Challenge

So, what are you waiting for? Buckle up. Do the work. GRIT isn't about being the best – it's about being the one who refuses to quit. Whether your "mountain" is a career, a dream, or a relationship, GRIT is the key to reaching the summit.

As a value-based leader, it's not just about your goals – it's about how you achieve them. Do you want to be the one who talks about their values, or the one who lives them?

Start now. Start here. And remember: The right choice is rarely the easy choice, but it's always worth it.

Chapter 5

Stress Management – From Enemy to Superpower

Stress isn't your enemy. Your unwillingness to manage it is the problem.

Stress. The word thrown around in every workplace, every management group, and in every article about work environment. But what is stress, really?

Stress isn't the malevolent force that ruins your life. In fact, stress is designed to save you.

Imagine the savanna. You're face-to-face with a saber-toothed tiger. Your body floods with cortisol and adrenaline. Your heart races. Your muscles tense. Your body prepares you to fight or flee like crazy.

But here's the issue: today, it's not tigers chasing us – it's deadlines, overflowing inboxes, and never-ending Teams meetings. The body reacts the same way. The cortisol flood overwhelms you, but no tiger ever appears.

Turning Stress Into a Superpower

Take Serena Williams, one of the greatest tennis players of all time. At the height of her career, she faced enormous pressure—not just on the court but also off it—with the media scrutinizing every step and the world holding unrealistic expectations.

During the 2015 US Open final, while chasing the rare achievement of winning all four Grand Slam titles in one year, Serena admitted afterward to feeling paralyzed by pressure and stress. Instead of giving in, she turned the stress into energy. She focused her mind and channeled the stress into an extraordinary performance, securing victory.

Serena has said: "I feel stress, but I've learned that it doesn't have to define me. It can lift me, if I let it."

Her story is a reminder that stress doesn't have to be your enemy. It can be your secret superpower – if you know how to manage it.

Why Stress Is Your Secret Superpower

Stress isn't inherently dangerous. Chronic stress is dangerous. The difference?

- **Short-term stress:** Sharpens focus. Boosts performance.
- **Chronic stress:** Weakens the immune system, disrupts sleep, and can lead to burnout.

So the question isn't, "How do I avoid stress?" but "How do I manage it?"

The Big Four of Stress Mastery – Champions' Techniques

Want to master stress? Try these four techniques:

1. Breath Control – Take Command of Your System
When your body starts stressing, the first thing that happens is shallow breathing.
  The trick? Let your breath take control.

Try "box breathing":
- Inhale for 5 seconds.
- Hold your breath for 5 seconds.
- Exhale for 5 seconds.
- Pause for 5 seconds.
Repeat this 5-10 times. It calms your nervous system instantly and reduces cortisol levels.

2. Self-Talk – Rewire Your Mental Script
How do you talk to yourself when the pressure's on?
- **„I've got this.“**
- "I've been in tough situations before."
- „I'm in control.“

What you say to yourself becomes your truth.

Replace negative thoughts with positive affirmations. Yes, it feels strange at first. But it works.

3. Visualization – Prepare Your Brain for Success
Athletes have used this for decades:

- Visualize a successful meeting.
- See yourself staying calm under pressure.
- Feel the sensation of being in control.

The brain can't distinguish between real and mental images. Train it to see yourself as a winner.

4. Goal Setting – Break Down the Chaos
Stress often feels like overwhelming chaos.
Solution?

- Break it down.
- **Split big goals into smaller steps.**
- Take one thing at a time.

Example: "Write the book" becomes → Write 200 words today.

Stress Traps – And How to Avoid Them

There are five classic stress traps. Do you recognize any of these?

1. Avoidance – "I'll Deal With It Later"

You put off an unpleasant task. The stress grows.
Solution: Handle it immediately. Tackle that nagging issue now.

2. Escape – "I Can't Deal With This"

You avoid the conflict. The stress lingers.
   Solution: Face what you're avoiding. It won't get easier later.

3. Minimizing – "It's Probably Not That Bad"

You suppress the feeling. But the stress doesn't go away—it turns into internal pressure.
Solution: Acknowledge that you're stressed. Then manage it.

4. Impatience – "I Have to Solve Everything NOW!"

Stress makes you hyperactive—but ineffective.
Solution: Slow down. Focus on one thing at a time.

5. Adrenaline Addiction – "I Work Best Under Pressure"

Yes, adrenaline can give you superpowers. But too much? Total system failure.
Solution: Use adrenaline for short bursts—not as a constant fuel.

How to Build Stress Resilience – Long-Term Strength

Want to get better at handling stress over time? Here are your keys:

- **Sleep:** Prioritize quality sleep—it's stress's best antidote.
- **Diet:** Stable blood sugar = a stable mind.
- **Exercise:** Physical activity clears out stress hormones.
- **Social Support:** Talk to people. Don't isolate yourself.

Conclusion: Stress Isn't Your Enemy – It's Your Teacher

Stress isn't something to avoid.
It's a signal. An indicator. A tool.
Learn to:

- Manage it **physically** (breathing and sleep).
- Manage it **mentally** (self-talk and goal setting).
- Manage it **long-term** (lifestyle choices).

You're stronger than you think. Stress isn't your enemy – you decide how it affects you.

Conclusion;

7 Brutally Honest Tips for Engagement and Results – No Excuses, Just Action

Do you want stronger results? Great. Then it's time to drop all half-hearted attempts and start playing for real. Engagement isn't something you feel – it's something you do.

Here are 7 tips that don't just boost your results – they push you to step out of your comfort zone.

1. Decide Who You Want to Become – Not Just What You Want to Achieve

Stop rambling about vague goals. Write down exactly what character traits you want to be known for.

Is it integrity? Then stop exaggerating and keep your promises.

Is it courage? Then stop postponing tough conversations and address them head-on.

Behavior always trumps words – every time.

2. Write Down Your Three Biggest "WHYs" – And Set Fire to Your Excuses

Why do you want that result? And no, "because it would be fun" isn't enough.

Write down three deeper reasons. What will you gain? What will you lose if you don't act?

A strong WHY keeps you going even when motivation dies.

A weak WHY leads to excuses.

3. Get a High-Performing Coach – Someone Who Won't Sugarcoat Things

Do you want results or sympathy?

Find someone who holds you accountable – a mentor, coach, or sparring partner.

Someone who asks uncomfortable questions and won't let you slide with, "I tried."

Be prepared to hear: "That's nonsense. Do the work."

4. Burn Your Bridges – Make Failure Unacceptable

Stop leaving the door open for excuses.

Remove all escape routes that give you an out.

Tell others what you're going to do – and let them hold you accountable.

When giving up becomes uncomfortable, you'll keep going.

5. Meet Inaction with Brutal Action – NOW!

Feeling tired? Motivation gone? Congratulations. Do it anyway.
    Action creates motivation – not the other way around.
    Start small, but start. Write one sentence. Do one push-up. Take ONE step.

Perfection is the enemy of action.

6. Eliminate the Word "Try" – Go All-in

"I'm going to try to exercise tomorrow."
    Stop.
    You either do it, or you don't.
    "Trying" is a preemptive excuse for not following through.

Do you want results? Commit – completely.

7. Create Energy – Because It's What Performance Demands

You can't deliver at your best if your body and brain are running on empty.
    Exercise. Not for the beach body – but for mental sharpness.
    Sleep. Because your brain needs recovery to perform.
    Eat. Properly. Cut out sugar crashes and sloppy habits.

Strong results start with strong energy.

Conclusion: How You Spend Your Time Reveals Who You Are

Want to know what someone truly prioritizes?
    Look at where they spend their time.
    Look at how they use their money.

Engagement isn't about words. It's about action.

Do you want to play big? Start acting like the person you want to become – now.

Summary of Part 1: Leading Yourself

The Foundations of Self-Leadership

Leading yourself is the first and most essential building block of leadership. Part 1 highlights how self-awareness, character, and courage create a strong internal foundation. When you learn to navigate your strengths, weaknesses, and values, you can face the world with stability and clarity.

Keys to Leading Yourself:

1. **Self-Awareness and Character:** Understand your values and let them guide your decisions. A strong character is the backbone of authentic leadership.
2. **Mental and Physical Strength:** Your energy and resilience drive you forward. Take care of your health and train your mind to handle pressure and uncertainty.
3. **The Art of Change:** Adaptability is crucial. Grow through challenges and guide your team through the four phases of change.
4. **Values and Self-Discipline:** Live by your values, even when no one is watching. Self-discipline is the tool to achieve your goals.
5. **Stress Management and Balance:** Transform stress from an enemy into a superpower. With the right strategies, you can use stress to grow and perform better.

An Inspiring Reminder:

Leadership always starts with you. Just like Alexander the Great led with action rather than words, you can be a role model by living your values. It's not about perfection—it's about persistence and courage to keep moving forward.

Conclusion:

When you lead yourself with self-awareness and integrity, you create a solid foundation to lead others and build successful organizations. Ask yourself: What can I do today to become a stronger and more authentic leader? Your answer is the starting point for the next step in your journey. Let's go!

Reflection Questions for Leading Yourself:

1. What are your most central values, and how are they reflected in your daily decisions?
2. How do you currently handle stress and challenges? Is there a strategy from this book you can start using to strengthen your inner leadership?
3. When was the last time you faced a change? How did you navigate through the four phases of change described in the book?
4. How balanced is your mental, physical, and emotional health? What can you do to strengthen this balance?
5. In what ways can you demonstrate greater self-discipline to achieve your long-term goals, and what small steps can you take starting today?

Appendix: The Character Matrix

Build Your House on Solid Ground

Exercise: The Character Matrix

If you need guidance through the process, you can watch three short films that result in a complete personal blueprint, including your character matrix. Download the character matrix and print an image of who you are today—while simultaneously sketching the vision of the person you want to be in the future.

Visit: https://charactermatrix.strongresults.se

Alternatively, you can choose from one of the 21 options provided or select your own word along with the behavior required to embody it. Use what resonates with you the most.

Alternative;

21 Infallible Qualities/Abilities for a Leader

Prioritization/Ranking/Definitions/Explanations

(Overlaps between qualities are not an issue; it's often an advantage.)

1. **Belief in Success/Visionary:** A platform to help you see further ahead. Long-term oriented. Prioritizes strategy over short-term tactics. Sees opportunities before obstacles. Open to improvement. Adaptable and constantly learning. Recognizes Darwin's first law: "An organism that does not evolve at the pace of or faster than its surroundings dies!"—a principle that applies to people, too.

2. **Competence:** Knowledgeable, constantly learning, and improving. Not only do you possess knowledge, but you also know how to apply

it. Aware of your strengths and confident. Familiar with your field and industry, allowing you to innovate and grow new business opportunities.

3. **Responsible:** You take ownership of your tasks, obligations, and commitments. Never shifting blame or avoiding issues—problems are there to be solved. You protect your team and take responsibility for their potential failures. Quality thinking is part of your mental toolkit.

4. **Engaged/Present:** You pause, reflect, and focus. You are passionate about your tasks, embrace challenges, and prioritize the company's success over your own. You stick to long-term strategies instead of chasing short-term tactical wins. You involve your team early in projects.

5. **Humorous/Detached:** You can laugh at yourself and your flaws. Humor provides a valuable perspective that helps you see things as they are. While you take issues and projects seriously, you don't necessarily take yourself too seriously. Humor is an underrated quality, potentially one of the most effective leadership tools.

6. **Action-Oriented:** Dynamic, energetic, courageous, and proactive. You take initiative without waiting for directives. You have the courage to make decisions and stick to them even in tough situations. You don't sit idly until opportunities pass. Civil courage and fearlessness in conflict are key traits.

7. **Attentive/Empathetic:** You listen, learn, and develop. A team player who adapts to the times. Inclusive, perceptive, understanding, approachable, and attentive to employees' questions and issues.

8. **Holistic Thinker:** You see the big picture before the details. Prioritize the team over the individual. Favor long-term solutions over short-term "firefighting." You prefer playing the chess game over being a pawn controlled by others.

9. **Solution-Oriented:** You find solutions to problems instead of dwelling on the problems themselves. Highly adaptable, following Darwin's second law: It's not the strongest or smartest but the most adaptable that wins. You are quick, competent, and efficient, considering both the whole picture and its consequences.

10. **Goal-Oriented/Focused:** Prioritize one path or activity over many. Laser focus rather than a lightbulb (which leaks energy). You prioritize important tasks over urgent ones. Decisive, consistent, and not afraid of conflict.

11. **Creative:** Flexible and open to ideas. Creativity doesn't necessarily mean innovation; it can also involve combining existing knowledge in new ways. And if you're among the 5% who can bring ideas to fruition, you're among those who drive companies forward.

12. **Analytical:** Methodical and systematic. This might sound dull, but it doesn't have to turn into defensive maintenance. Well-founded theories help you tackle setbacks while ensuring success. Thoroughness is also part of your mental toolkit.

13. **Efficient:** You excel at multitasking and achieve much in little time. Your ability to deliver relies heavily on your talent for prioritization. You are productive, don't waste energy unnecessarily, and ensure that your input outweighs leaks like frustrations or unresolved issues.

14. **Straightforward:** Reliable, consistent, and honest. You do what you say, take action, and follow through. You are dependable, secure, and honorable. Recognizing that lies undermine both self-esteem and focus, you aim to remain truthful.

15. **Fair/Independent:** Balancing personal interests with broader ones. You enjoy seeing others grow. You prioritize the team over yourself, often staying in the background and letting others take the credit.

16. **Loyal/Solidarity-Driven:** You are 100% loyal to your organization and team. Never throwing others under the bus, you may even take blame for problems you didn't cause. You protect the brand and expand your responsibilities rather than shy away from them.

17. **Resourceful/Profit-Driven:** You prioritize profitability as it enables organizational freedom. Focus on revenue over expenses, hard work over avoiding challenges. Smart prioritization is also part of your toolkit.

18. **Competitive:** Energetic and driven by competition. Balancing this energy with patience is critical; impatience can be your biggest enemy, while your drive is your greatest ally.

19. **Entrepreneurial:** Active and full of energy. You take initiative, continually moving forward. You drive change and embrace challenges without hesitation, relinquishing any focus on titles or excessive personnel management.

20. **Winner:** You see opportunities in everything. A risk-taker who approaches challenges head-on, like successful slalom skiers grazing the gates. You refuse to settle for second place and aren't afraid to rewrite rules or reallocate resources to gain an edge.

21. **Smart:** Goal-oriented and skilled at aligning tactics with long-term strategies. Your competitive intelligence is paired with an ability to assess people's character, using their strengths to achieve positive outcomes and ambitious goals. While this may sound manipulative, as long as your purpose is good, it's the foundation of building winning teams.

Red Lines

And for the Red Line, here are 7 qualities to choose from, or you can select your own word. **Red Lines** are like a double-edged sword. A strong resource but one that can lead you into trouble if you're not aware of it.

Choose only one.

1. Impatient

- The most prominent "negative" trait, as it can easily translate into decisiveness, drive, and entrepreneurial spirit.
- *(A double-edged sword that needs careful balancing.)*

2. Stubborn

- Explained as persistent, goal-oriented.

3. Passive/Preserver

- Explained as thoughtful, reliable, secure, and responsible.

4. Defensive/Cowardly

- Explained as thoughtful, secure, reliable, and responsible. Waiting to avoid unnecessary risks.

5. Risk-Taker

- A necessary trait for development. The alternative is stagnation and the slow death of the company.

6. Cynical/Cold-Hearted

- Prefers rational solutions over emotional ones. Prioritizes the company's best interest. Clear thinking enhances this.

7. Self-Centered

- Explained as goal-focused, determined, decisive, and confident.

Part 2: Leading Others

Introduction

Leading Like Lao Tzu – Towards Strong Results

Lao Tzu claimed that the best leader is the one who is barely noticed.

Excuse me, does that mean hiding behind a plant in the office? Of course not – it's about creating an environment where others shine, and where the results speak for themselves. Because when people feel they have control and ownership, and when they can proudly say, "That? We made it happen!", then you've succeeded. Paradoxically, it's when you let go of control that you truly gain it.

However, this requires something that many leaders prefer to avoid: trust and patience. Having the courage to stay silent when everyone expects you to step in. Allowing your team to make mistakes – and learn from them. This is not for those who love to dazzle during PowerPoint presentations or take all the applause at the weekly meeting. It's for the brave leader who dares to believe in the power of others.

Strong results require trust (and a pinch of humility)

Let's be honest: it's tempting to want control over everything and everyone. "If I just keep track of all the details, the results will shine." But Lao Tzu would probably say something like, "Relax, overworked manager, that will only create a pile of stress and mediocre results."

A values-based leader knows that success is built on clear principles, trust, and connection – not through micromanagement. Want a team that delivers at the highest level? Give them the space to think for themselves, the freedom to make decisions, and the responsibility to deliver. And when they succeed? Step aside and let them take the spotlight.

But it takes courage to let go of control. To trust that your employees will not only solve the problems but excel at them. Is it risky? Of course. Is it worth it? Absolutely.

The paradox of leadership – the less you're seen, the greater your impact

The greatest leader is not the one who is most visible. It is the one who, without being seen, shapes a culture where people take responsibility, grow, and do their absolute best. It's a paradox: The less you dominate, the more successful you become.

So here's the question: Are you creating an environment where your employees can proudly say, "We made this happen!"? If yes – congratulations, you've not only created strong results but also a legacy of trust and values that will live on long after you've moved on.

And isn't that what leadership is really about? Not just achieving results but building a culture where people reach their full potential – without you needing to wave a flag.

Leading others is not for the faint-hearted.

It's one of the most challenging and meaningful tasks we can undertake. It requires a balance between empathy and decisiveness, and sometimes it feels like navigating through a storm without a map. But when it succeeds – when trust is built, and the direction is clear – the reward is nothing less than transformational.

Because, in the end, it's this kind of leadership that doesn't just create successful teams – it also builds a better world.

Table of Contents

Chapter 1: Coaching and Employee Development – Unlocking Potential

Leading others begins with helping them grow. Coaching is about building awareness, accountability, and confidence to act. By listening, asking questions, and guiding, you can unlock the hidden potential in each individual.

The Four Pillars of Coaching

1. **Trust**: The foundation of effective coaching. Create an open and safe environment.
2. **Awareness**: Help employees identify their strengths and areas for development.
3. **Challenge**: Ask questions that inspire reflection and action.
4. **Hope**: Show belief in their ability to succeed and build their confidence.
5. Practical Tools

- Plan regular conversations with clear goals.
- Use open-ended questions to spark insights.
- Celebrate successes and reinforce positive behaviors.

Chapter 2: Communication and Conflict Management – Keys to Strong Relationships

Communication is the foundation of all relationships. A leader must both articulate clearly and listen actively. Conflicts are a natural part of work life and should be seen as opportunities for growth.

Effective Communication

1. Be clear, concrete, and responsive.
2. Use storytelling to create engagement and understanding.
3. Build trust through transparency and honesty.

Conflict Management in Three Steps

- Identify the problem: Focus on facts and specific situations.
- Listen with empathy: Give all parties space to share their perspectives.
- Create solutions: Collaborate to find a path forward that works for everyone.

Chapter 3: Team Development and Organizational Culture – Foundations for Success

Building strong teams and a healthy organizational culture is at the core of values-based leadership. A culture where people feel involved and inspired creates sustainable results.

Building a Strong Culture

- Highlight and train key people who embody the organization's values.
- Create meetings that not only solve problems but also strengthen team cohesion.
- Anchor your values through concrete examples and stories.

The Three Steps of Team Development

1. **Trust**: Develop an environment where employees feel safe to be themselves.
2. **Collaboration**: Create opportunities for everyone to contribute and take responsibility.
3. **Engagement**: Provide the team with a clear vision and goals to strive for.

Chapter 4: Motivation and Engagement – Helping Teams Thrive

Motivation is the driving force that takes a team from simply performing to truly excelling. By creating the right conditions, you can ignite engagement even in the most reluctant employees.

The Seven Keys to Motivation

1. Assign responsibilities that inspire.
2. Show appreciation for successes.
3. Create a clear vision everyone can rally around.
4. Offer development opportunities.
5. Provide the freedom to act and make decisions.
6. Build confidence by showing how their work makes a difference.
7. Address fears by creating a sense of security.

Avoid Motivation Killers

- Micromanagement and lack of clarity.
- Lack of accountability and follow-up.
- Stagnant tasks.

Chapter 5: Trust – The Core of Values-Based Leadership

Trust is the cornerstone of successful leadership. By combining strength and humility, you can create an environment where people dare to take responsibility and explore their potential.

Building Trust

1. Be consistent and live your values.
2. Communicate honestly and with integrity.
3. Show both strength and flexibility in your leadership.

The Power of Trust

4. Let the team feel your confidence in their abilities.
5. Encourage independent thinking and problem-solving.
6. Stand behind their decisions and provide support during setbacks.

Summary of Part 2: The Path to Leading Others

Leading others is about inspiring, building relationships, and creating a culture where people dare to grow. Through coaching, communication, team development, motivation, and trust, you lay the foundation for sustainable success – not only for the team but for the entire organization.

From Top-Down Management to Values-Based Leadership

Top-down management is dead. Long live values-based leadership! Today's workforce has simply had enough of old hierarchical models where the carrot-and-stick approach ruled. Spoiler: it's 2025, and it's time to realize that people want to work with their hearts, minds, and a clear sense of purpose – not just because "the boss said so."

An inspiring leadership journey is the one Paul Polman, former CEO of Unilever, embarked on. When he stepped in as the leader of the company, he decided to challenge the status quo. Instead of focusing on short-term profits and shareholder demands, he introduced the "Unilever Sustainable Living Plan" – a long-term vision that put the planet, people, and sustainability at the center. It was a radical move that made both investors and the industry take notice.

Polman believed in running a business driven by values. He understood that the talent of the future didn't just want to work for a company that made profits – they wanted to create meaningful change. By communicating a clear vision, giving teams autonomy, and showing trust, Polman not only improved Unilever's results but also inspired an entire generation of leaders to think differently.

His journey shows that values-based leadership isn't just a modern trend. It's a way to create lasting success in a world where employees demand authenticity and purpose.

Let's talk about the younger generation – yes, those "millennials" and "Gen Zs" who often hear they're lazy (but fortunately don't listen to that nonsense). Here's what they actually are:

- **More independent:** They'd rather Google something than ask you.

- **Quicker to find solutions on their own:** A "problem" is just a YouTube tutorial away.

- **More critical of authority:** They don't buy into "this is how we've always done it" – sorry, but that's so 1995.

Want these brilliant yet questioning individuals to perform at their best? Then you need to give them something that fires them up: clear values, a purpose they can feel, and goals that go beyond "more Excel reports." Because honestly, who runs faster to fill out another column?

Building Future Leaders – Here's the Deal

You need to let go. Yes, it's scary, but that's exactly what's required. Here's what you should ditch (and what to embrace instead):

- **Control for trust:** If you need to micromanage every detail, you're either doing it wrong – or don't trust your team.

- **Micromanagement for accountability:** Give people the space to shine. They might even surprise you (in a good way!).

- **Slow three-year plans for agile adaptation:** Sorry, but the world is changing faster than you can say "strategy meeting." Adaptability is the new leadership.

So here's the thing: If you don't want to be the leader your employees avoid in the hallway, it's time to wake up. Leave the control-driven culture behind and step into a world where values lead and trust is the currency. It might sound risky – but the biggest risk right now is not daring to change.

Chapter 1

Coaching and Employee Development

*"Building awareness, accountability, drive, and confidence to act!
That is the goal of coaching."*

In the early 1990s, I moved to Oslo for love.

I didn't know anyone besides my girlfriend – and yes, let's just say that "spontaneous socializing" wasn't exactly a thing on my calendar. So what do you do? You sign up for the gym, of course. The gym quickly became my second home, and it was there that I met Mark.

An Australian with as much energy as a caffeine-fueled kangaroo and a passion for training that almost made me tired just listening to him.

Mark had lived in both Australia and the USA and knew everything there was to know about personal training. The problem? Nobody in Scandinavia knew what personal training was. When he suggested we start a business, I initially thought he was crazy. But Mark wasn't just persuasive – he was a master at coaching. He saw potential in me long before I saw it in myself.

A memorable moment:

We were sitting in the gym's reception area in central Oslo, drinking coffee (again), and Mark asked me:

– "Of all the people who walk through this door, do you think that with your experience and personality, **you can help 80% of them achieve better results**?"

I stared at him as if he had just suggested I climb Mount Everest barefoot.

– "Maybe," I replied hesitantly.

Mark smiled. He leaned in and said, with that voice only a true coach can have:

– "Then **why don't you believe in yourself**?"

BOOM. That hit me like a dumbbell to the head. And you know what? I started to believe. With Mark's coaching, I filled my calendar with clients, even though I was still studying full-time. Within a few months, I was training over 120 clients a month. It was like suddenly realizing I could not only climb over obstacles – I could leap over them.

But here's the most important thing: It was never about me. It was about the process.

Coaching is about helping others grow, moving from point A to point B. It's not your background, experience, or charm that makes the difference. It's your ability to ask the right questions, listen, and guide.

What does it take to coach at an elite level?

Let's be honest: It's not easy, but it's also not impossible. The secret? Leave your ego at the door. **Coaching isn't about you – it's about the other person**. Your role is to highlight their strengths, help them see their potential, and guide them to take action.

And if you doubt whether you can do it? Remember this: If I, as a 1990s student in a gym in Oslo, could learn to coach – so can you. Start with one question:

"How can I help this person take their next step?

The Art of Coaching Team Members

What is the most important mission of leadership?

It's a question that should hang like a painting in every leader's office, engraved in every boardroom, and whispered as a mantra in every team meeting. What is it that we're really doing? The answer is both simple and monumental: To **create results through others**.

But let's be honest – this is often where things go wrong. Leadership isn't about being the constant fixer, nor is it about taking on the world's problems and burning yourself out. No, your job is to make others **want to** – and **be able to** – **action**. So how do you do that?

The Three Pillars of Leadership

If we simplify it down to the basics (because everything is easier with lists), leadership is about three things:

1. **Leading yourself** – If you can't lead yourself, how can you lead anyone else?
2. **Leading others** – Coaching is at the heart of this. It's not just a method; it's a mindset.
3. **Leading the organization** – Nobody likes goal-setting… until they see what happens without it.

It's simple in theory. But then we step into reality, where 2023 Gallup statistics hit us like a cold shower:

- **24%** of employees are disengaged – actively or passively working against everything you're trying to achieve.
- **63%** are coasting – doing just enough not to stand out, and definitely no more.
- **13%** are driving forward – they're the heroes, carrying the team on their shoulders.

So if you have a team of ten people: Two are pulling in the wrong direction, six are just sitting there watching, and one lonely hero is pedaling forward. The problem? If you do nothing, you'll soon lose the one person who's actually pedaling.

Performance Reviews as a Tool – Not a Waste of Time

We all know that performance reviews are hated by many managers and loved by HR. Most see it as a ritual without much meaning – like filling out a survey. But what if you saw it instead as your golden opportunity to coach and create momentum?

Use the conversation to introduce a new mindset: **urgency.** There's no better word for the sense of drive, focus, that every business needs – especially now, when pandemics and remote work have eroded much of the workplace morale. It's time to wake up the team.

The Four Steps of Coaching to Turn Things Around

Step 1: Build Trust

No coaching tool in the world works without trust. And no, trust isn't built by being the loudest in the room or always being right. It's about listening. Really listening. Find common ground, share a bit of yourself (yes, even your weaknesses – people love that). Create a sense of "we" that makes the employee feel safe to open up. Without this? You're just a boss giving orders.

Step 2: Raise Awareness

95% of our thoughts and decisions are subconscious. It's like driving a car without knowing where you're going. Your job is to help the employee become aware of their current situation and where they genuinely want to go. Spend half of the coaching time here. Ask questions like:

- Where are you right now, and why?
- What are you most proud of?
- What are the consequences if you choose not to act?
- If you were to take ONE step from here, what would it be?
- What would the benefits be if you "arrived"?
- What would it mean for you in the long term?

Pause until you see the spark light up. Only when they truly understand their current situation and start visualizing their ideal future can they begin to shape their path forward.

Step 3: Challenge

Once you have the employee's trust and they're aware of their current situation, it's time to apply pressure. We all "end up in the ditch" from time to time when building new habits and behaviors. This is where the strength lies – they've already told you where they are, what they want to do, and why. That's why it's relatively easy to challenge them.
  Ask questions like:

- What do you really want?
- What made you decide to take action here?
- What benefits did you see if you started acting?
- What are you willing to do to get there?
- How will you ensure you actually do it – not just think about it?

This is where many leaders chicken out. They don't want to seem "mean" or "pushy." But if you don't challenge, how will the employee reach their full potential? You're not there to be popular – you're there to create results.

Step 4: Feed Them Hope and Confidence

Here comes the cheerleader. People need to believe that success is possible – otherwise, they'll never take action. You need to be the one who sees their potential, even when they don't. Build their confidence, but also give them the tools to succeed. And never forget: You're there to lift, not carry.

Summary: How Do You Prepare Their Skis?

Leading is like waxing skis. Some employees need more grip – security and stability to dare to move forward. Others need more glide – freedom and inspiration to maximize their drive. Your job is to figure out who needs what and tailor your coaching accordingly.

And finally, a reminder: Leadership is always about creating results through others. You're not the one who's supposed to pedal the fastest – you're the one who's supposed to get the whole team moving.

Chapter 2.

Communication and Conflict Management – The Key to Strong Relationships

The art of influencing others – and actually getting them to listen

Communication is, without a doubt, one of the most underrated superpowers in the world.

We communicate all the time – with words, body language, silences, and even through that frustrated look when the PowerPoint presentation crashes. But let's be honest: how many of us are truly good at communicating? Really good – at influencing, engaging, and making people think, "Wow, this person has something important to say."

To succeed, you don't just need to talk – you need to create influence. You need to make people not just hear you, but actually listen. It's an art form. So, what's the secret? How do you become a master at influencing others, getting them to buy into your ideas, follow your guidance, and maybe even applaud after a meeting?

An inspiring example of the power of communication is Martin Luther King Jr.'s iconic "I Have a Dream" speech. On a warm August day in 1963, he gathered over 250,000 people at the Lincoln Memorial in Washington, D.C., and changed the course of history. He knew it wasn't enough to simply talk about equality – he needed to make people feel it in their hearts.

King used powerful imagery and passionate language to paint a vision of the future. He didn't just say what he believed – he showed what the world could look like if people followed his vision. His repetition of the phrase "I have a dream" created a rhythm that embedded itself deep in people's consciousness. It wasn't just a speech; it was an experience.

What can we learn from him? Communication isn't just about words. It's about creating an emotional connection, showing your conviction, and using your voice to inspire action. King built trust through his clarity and authenticity – he lived the values he preached, and that's why people listened.

The eternal question: Trust or fear?

Back in the Renaissance, Machiavelli posed the classic question in *The Prince*: "Is it better to be loved than feared, or vice versa?" His answer? "It is much safer to be feared than loved." Okay, we can agree it worked for him (and maybe for a few tyrants throughout history), but let's be realistic. In today's world, leadership isn't about creating fear – it's about building trust. Because without trust, you have nothing. People won't listen, follow, or care.

And yet, trust isn't something you can just demand. It's something you have to earn. It's like trying to balance a plate of spaghetti on your head – it requires focus, skill, and a lot of practice.

Seven Keys to Influence

1. **Trust – The foundation of everything**
    Want to influence someone? Start by building trust. Without it, you're going nowhere. Trust is about authenticity – being real. People need to feel that you're reliable, that you do what you say, and that you actually care. But here's the tricky part: trust is fragile. It can take years to build but be shattered in a second (think of that time you "accidentally" missed a meeting and blamed it on not seeing the email).
    How do you build trust? By showing a part of yourself. Not the perfect version, but the human one. Nobody likes a too-polished facade – it feels as trustworthy as a used car dealer promising, "It's barely been driven."
2. **Charm – An energy giver, not an energy thief**
    Charm isn't about being the loudest person in the room or cracking the funniest jokes. It's about giving energy, not taking it. You know, those

people who make you feel comfortable, important, and heard. That's charm. Want to develop it? Learn to listen. No, I mean really listen. Not the "I'm-just-waiting-for-my-turn-to-talk" kind of listening, but genuine listening.

3. **Genuine interest – It's not about you**
    Here's a hard truth: most people don't care about you. They care about themselves. And that's okay – it's human. Want to influence someone? Show that you care about them. Ask questions, listen to their answers, and build relationships that aren't about what you want. As Harvey Mackay said, "People buy from people they like." This applies not just to products – but to ideas, visions, and leadership.

4. **Knowledge and expertise – Never stop learning**
    Want long-term influence? Then you need to show that you're competent. And no, this doesn't mean you have to know everything (nobody likes a know-it-all). It means continuously developing, learning, and improving yourself. People follow those who are experts but also those who show they're willing to grow. What skill will you sharpen over the next six months?

5. **Strong character – Do what you say you'll do**
    Integrity is the foundation of all influence. People follow those who practice what they preach. If you say you'll do something – do it. If you claim to stand for something – stand for it, even when it's hard. It's simple in theory, but so many fail in practice.

6. **Avoid energy thieves – Arrogance, know-it-all attitudes, and ingratitude**
    These are the death of influence. Arrogant people may gain power, but they rarely keep it. The same goes for know-it-alls who never let anyone else be right. And ingratitude? It's like dropping a grenade in the room – it destroys everything.

7. **Be proactive – See opportunities, not obstacles**
    The most influential people are those who look forward, not backward. Those who talk about solutions, not problems. Those who radiate hope and faith in the future. Influence is about being a guiding light – someone others want to follow, not because they have to, but because they want to.

Rhetoric and Argumentation Techniques

The Art of Persuasion – and Doing It Like a Master

There's a crucial difference between talking and actually being heard. We've all been there – listening to someone who seems to talk forever but leaves us with absolutely nothing, or that time we tried to convince others and were met with blank, empty stares from our audience. So, what's the secret to arguing and persuading successfully?

Here's the truth: Your ability to argue is the difference that makes the difference. This applies whether you're trying to sell an idea to your team, win a discussion with your partner at home, or pitch a solution to your clients. And just like anything else – preparation is the key. It's not your charisma or charm that wins; it's your ability to be prepared, structured, and relevant.

A brilliant example of the power of argumentation techniques is the story of Malala Yousafzai. After surviving a brutal attack by the Taliban for her fight for girls' right to education, she stood before a global audience at the UN in 2013. Despite her young age and enormous pressure, Malala demonstrated masterful rhetoric. She used her story, her passion, and her clear structure to make the world's leaders listen.

Malala said: "One pen and one book can change the world." With simple but powerful words, she painted a vision of what was at stake. She used her personal experience to create an emotional connection and supported her message with facts and a clear call to action. It wasn't just what she said, but how she said it – her rhetorical skill combined with genuine conviction made her words resonate long after the speech was over.

Her performance reminds us that argumentation isn't just about winning a discussion. It's about changing minds, creating momentum, and inspiring action. Malala's story is proof that with the right technique and a clear conviction, your voice can reach and influence even the largest arenas.

The Foundations of Argumentation: Preparation and Structure

If there's one thing you should take away from this, let it be this: 80% of your success lies in preparation. It's about knowing what you want to say, why you want to say it, and how it resonates with the recipient. Here's a simple but powerful model to help you build your arguments:

FAB -Model:

- **F** stands for **features**: What are you presenting? It could be a product, an idea, or a change – what it is, what it can do, and how it works.

- **A** stand for **Advantages**: And advantages for whom? The recipient.

- **B** stands for **Benefit**: What's the benefit for the recipient? What do they gain from it? What do they save? What do they avoid?

The most common mistake is getting stuck on features – what the product, idea, or change is or does. Nobody cares about that unless you link it to what it does for the recipient, focusing on their benefits and value. **Save, gain, or avoid** – that's the key.

The Rhetorical Structure: Build Your Message Like a Masterpiece

Want to truly convince others? Then you need a structure that functions like an architectural masterpiece. Here's how to build it:

- **Introduction**: Grab attention. It could be a question, an anecdote, or a surprising fact. Make your audience want to hear more.

- **Background**: Set the scene. Why is this relevant? What brought us here? Build understanding. Background is about "placing the ball on the penalty spot" so you can score with your main message.

81

- **Main Message (thesis):** What's the core idea? What do you want to say? Be clear and concise.

- **Arguments:** Here's your chance to prove that what you're saying is true. This is where the FAB model shines.

- **Address Objections:** This is the masterstroke. Consider what objections people might have – and address them before they even ask.

- **Conclusion:** Summarize powerfully and leave your audience with a clear "call-to-action" or something to ponder.

Presentation Techniques for Leaders: Where Rhetoric Meets Reality

Mastering presentation techniques is an art that requires more than just content. It's about how you deliver – about creating a bond with your audience, inspiring them, and leaving an impression that lingers long after you've finished speaking.

A brilliant example of the power of presentation techniques is the story of Steve Jobs and his legendary product launches. When he introduced the first iPhone in 2007, he didn't just change how we view technology – he also demonstrated what a masterful presentation is all about. Jobs understood that a good presentation isn't just about informing – it's about captivating.

With simplicity and precision, he took his audience on a journey. He used clear visuals and graphic elements, stuck to three main points, and gradually built anticipation by saying: "Today, Apple is going to reinvent the phone." His delivery was confident, his language simple, and his passion for what he presented was contagious. Jobs showed that a presentation is more than just facts – it's an experience.

What can we learn from him? Successful presentations aren't about overwhelming the audience with information. They're about creating an emotional connection, making things easy to understand, and most importantly, inspiring people.

1. Preparation is everything

You would never board a plane where the pilot says, "I think I know the way." The same goes for your presentation. Use the **3H model**:

- **What do you want them to know?** (Head)
- **What do you want them to feel?** (Heart)
- **What do you want them to do?** (Hand)

By thinking in these three dimensions, you ensure your presentation touches on the rational, emotional, and actionable.

2. Know your audience

You wouldn't talk about the stock market to a kindergarten class, would you? Tailor your communication to your audience. What do they care about? What are their challenges? Speak their language.

3. Body language and voice

Your body language often says more than your words. Be open, maintain eye contact, and use gestures to emphasize your points. And your voice? Vary your pace and tone. Monotony is the death of a presentation.

4. Visualize your points

A picture says more than a thousand words – but only if the picture is clear. Keep your presentations simple and clean. Avoid text-heavy slides that make people yawn before you even start.

5. Handle nervousness

Everyone gets nervous. The difference is that the best handle it like a pro. Practice, breathe, and remember – the audience isn't there to judge you. They want you to succeed.

6. Engage your audience

Ask questions, share stories, and make them feel involved. Nobody likes being bombarded with facts – make it lively!

7. End with power

Summarize your main points and leave your audience with something to think about or act on. What you say last is often what they'll remember best – make it memorable.

Summary: The Art of Rhetoric is Your Key to Success

Argumentation techniques and rhetoric aren't just for politicians or lawyers – they're for anyone who wants to influence and inspire. Your structure, preparation, and ability to read your audience are what separate a good presentation from an unforgettable one.

So next time you stand in front of a group, ask yourself: Am I here to talk – or to connect and persuade? If it's the latter, then you know exactly what to do. Use FAB, build your rhetorical structure, and deliver like a master.

Because, as with everything in life: It's not what you say that matters – it's what they hear, feel, and believe.

Handling Conflicts

"You can't stop the waves, but you can learn to surf." — Jon Kabat-Zinn
Conflicts are a natural part of relationships and leadership. For a values-based leader, it's not about avoiding conflicts – it's about addressing them with courage, clarity, and a willingness to foster understanding. Conflicts can be uncomfortable, but they are also an opportunity to create clarity and build stronger relationships.

Conflicts: A Moldy Sandwich We Must Address

Conflicts are like a cheese sandwich with mold hidden under the butter. You can spread on more butter and hope no one notices the problem, but it doesn't change what's underneath. Sooner or later, the whole sandwich becomes inedible. That's exactly how conflicts work. If we ignore them, they grow and spread. Handling conflicts means taking out the knife, scraping away the mold, and addressing what everyone sees but no one dares to talk about. It's uncomfortable, yes, but it's also necessary.

An inspiring example of the importance of handling conflicts comes from Howard Schultz, the founder and CEO of Starbucks. When Schultz returned to the company during a crisis in 2008, he discovered that the corporate culture had lost its focus. Relationships between management and employees were strained, and communication was marked by uncertainty and avoidance of problems.

Schultz chose not to sweep the problems under the rug. He organized a series of open forums where employees at all levels of the company could share their honest opinions about what had gone wrong. He didn't just listen; he took the criticism to heart and began reshaping the culture from the ground up. One example was that he openly admitted his own mistakes as a leader and encouraged his team to do the same.

This strategy not only built bridges between management and employees – it also inspired renewed energy and a sense of shared responsibility. By handling the conflicts with courage and clarity, Schultz not only saved Starbucks but also restored trust within the organization.

Clarity – A Values-Based Leader's Weapon

Clarity is key in conflict management. A values-based leader knows that vague statements and half-hearted attempts at solutions often make the situation worse. Instead, concrete communication and honesty are required.

For example, if you need to address a missed deadline with a colleague, don't just say: "We need to get better at meeting deadlines." That's too general and leads nowhere. Instead, say: "I noticed we missed the deadline on the last project. Can we talk about what happened and how we can avoid it in the future?"

This type of clarity isn't about placing blame. It's about creating understanding and building trust for the future.

Three Steps to Handling Conflicts

1. **Identify the Problem**: Pinpoint what the conflict is really about. Is it a specific event, unclear expectations, or a behavioral pattern that needs to be addressed? Be concrete and fact-focused.

2. **Listen with Openness**: Give all parties the opportunity to share their perspectives. A values-based leader listens actively and without prejudice. Understanding isn't built by waiting for your turn to speak – it's built by truly hearing what others are saying.
3. **Find Solutions Together**: Conflicts aren't about winning or losing. They're about finding solutions that work for everyone. This is your way, and this is my way. Ask: "What can we do moving forward to find a common path for all of us?"

A Final Reflection

Handling conflicts isn't an art, it's a craft. It takes courage, clarity, and a willingness to be uncomfortable at times. But the rewards are enormous: stronger relationships, better teams, and an environment where people feel free to be themselves. A values-based leader sees conflicts not as obstacles but as opportunities to create long-term success.

So the next time you see a moldy sandwich, grab the knife. You'll not only thank yourself later – your team will too.

"Don't let the fear of losing be greater than the excitement of winning." — Robert Kiyosaki

Chapter 3.

Team Development and Organizational Culture – The Foundation for Success

A farmer decided to sow seeds.

As he sowed, some of the seeds fell along the path, and birds came and ate them. Some seeds fell on rocky ground, where there wasn't much soil. The seeds sprouted quickly, but they soon withered in the hot sun and died. Other seeds fell among thorn bushes, which choked the plants and prevented them from growing and producing ripe grain. But some seeds fell on good soil and yielded thirty times what was sown, some sixty, and some a hundred times as much.

This is more than just a story – it's a reflection of organizational culture. For a values-based leader, it's not just about leading people but about creating the right conditions for the team to grow and thrive. The question is: What does the good soil look like in your organization? And perhaps more importantly, how do you ensure that everyone in the organization understands the value of cultivating and nurturing it?

Metaphors can help us understand.

In the wonderful movie *Being There*, a simple gardener becomes an advisor to the American president. His advice, "In a garden, you have to tend to the seasons, or the garden will never bear fruit," is a reminder that leadership requires patience, strategy, and timing. To create a flourishing organizational culture, we must both nurture and wait.

The Same Color on the Shirts (SCOT's mentality)

– Creating a Culture of Collaboration and Accountability

"The best time to plant a tree was 20 years ago. The second best time is now."

What does that really mean? It's about building a strong and well-established foundation – now, today. It's about ensuring that your team isn't just playing the same game but is also playing for the same goal – **the same color on the shirts (SCOT's).**

SCOT's isn't just a catchphrase; it's a philosophy. It's the habit of acting in alignment with the organization's core values, from top to bottom. It ensures that everyone knows who does what and when. And it's not about titles; it's about building a team where everyone pulls in the same direction.

An inspiring example of this comes from Nelson Mandela's leadership during the 1995 Rugby World Cup in South Africa. Mandela saw sports as a way to unite a divided nation. Even though rugby had previously symbolized apartheid for many, Mandela donned the team's green jersey shirt and stood alongside the players. He understood the power of symbols and collaboration to foster unity.

By wearing the same color jersey as the team, he sent a powerful message: South Africa is one team, and every citizen plays an important role. His actions demonstrated that true leadership is about inspiring others to believe in a shared goal and working together to achieve it.

Creating SCOT's isn't just about everyone agreeing – it's about fostering a culture where differences are turned into strengths, and where every individual feels like part of something bigger. It's a philosophy that builds bridges, not walls.

Let's start with an example – a classic from the workplace: IT vs. Business.

When IT and Business Play Different Games

You've seen it before: The business side wants quick solutions, and IT tries to balance to-do lists longer than a Christmas wish list. It's as if they're playing two entirely different sports. Here are five classic examples of how things go wrong – from both sides:

Business Side:

1. Locks in the budget too early: The budget is set before needs are even clear, causing conflicts later on.
2. Blames IT for failures: If a project doesn't meet expectations, they point fingers without reflecting on their own role.
3. Demands everything but uses little: What's ordered is often larger than what's actually needed.
4. Changes without a consequence analysis: Project changes rarely lead to updated budgets or plans.
5. Avoids understanding their needs: They don't take the time to understand the problems and expect IT to solve them.

IT Department:

1. Delivers vague estimates: Time and cost projections are based on insufficient information, causing problems later.
2. Measures the wrong things: Focus is on technical details instead of creating business value.
3. Overprioritizes technology: The latest tech becomes more important than solving the real problem.
4. Lack of respect within the team: Developers, testers, and analysts look down on each other's roles.
5. Communicates without a business focus: Explains technical solutions without connecting them to business needs.

So, how do we break down the barriers?

The first step is to stop seeing the business side as the customer and IT as the supplier. Instead, they form a joint team that reports directly to management. They share the same goals, the same responsibilities, and – of course – the **same color on the shirts.**

It's about creating a culture where accountability isn't optional. Where collaboration is standard, and where everyone understands that the only way to win is to play as a team.

Four Steps to Strengthen Your Organizational Culture

1. Key Values-Based People (KVP)

If you want to build a sustainable organizational culture, start by identifying your Key Values-Based People (1-3 individuals). These people are more than just employees – torchbearers of your core values. Their role is crucial for establishing and reinforcing values-based leadership.

Finding and developing these individuals requires focus and awareness. But once they are in place, they form the foundation of your organization. With their support, almost nothing can shake the core values that define your organization's soul.

KVPs are also essential for setting the tone within the organization. By highlighting their actions and engagement, you create role models that others in the team can be inspired by. Remember, leadership isn't just about delegating – it's also about modeling the behavior and values you want to see in the organization.

2. Meetings That Inspire

Every meeting is an opportunity to reinforce your core values. Instead of just running through the agenda, start with 3-5 minutes focused on something that reflects your culture. It could be a story, a short video, or an insight from the past week. Also, give the team a chance to contribute by rotating responsibility for these minutes. Over time, you'll be amazed by the creativity and energy this generates.

Meetings aren't just about solving problems – they're platforms to remind everyone why you do what you do and what truly matters. Reflect on this: When was the last time you used a meeting to celebrate a small success or highlight someone who fully embodies your values? Small gestures like these can have a tremendous impact on team engagement.

3.   Your "WHY" Behind the Values

Values without a clear "why" are like a map without a compass. It's our "why" that motivates us to overcome obstacles and challenges. As a values-based leader, it's your responsibility to regularly remind the team why these values matter. Why did you choose this path? What are you striving for?

When people understand the deeper purpose behind your values, they become not only more motivated but also more engaged and resilient. One way to anchor this "why" is by connecting it to specific stories. For example: How has one of your core values helped you overcome a challenge or create success? Stories have a unique power to create connections and reinforce the meaning behind your choices.

The Soul of the Company and the Price of Productivity

SEB's Chairman of the board, Marcus Wallenberg has spoken of the "soul of the company" – a reminder that a strong organizational culture is the foundation of long-term success. This is supported by a 2018 Gallup poll in the U.S., which showed that more than two-thirds of employees were disengaged at work. This lack of engagement cost companies approximately $500 billion in lost productivity.

This demonstrates that without a vibrant company culture that engages, inspires, and guides employees, organizations lose more than just money – they lose their soul.

4. Individual Check-Ins

Ken Blanchard describes in *The One Minute Manager* the importance of regular, brief check-ins. As a leader, it's not about giving long lectures but asking insightful questions that help employees reflect on their actions and goals. Ask: "What do you think we can do better?" or "How do you think we are living up to our values?"

By creating space for self-reflection, you place responsibility where it belongs – with the individual. This is key to building a culture where everyone feels involved and accountable. Don't forget that regular check-ins not only strengthen the individual but also build trust and relationships between leaders and employees.

Thriving Organizational Cultures

Petter Stordalen (the hotel magnate) puts it well: "You can copy strategies and marketing plans, but you can never copy a culture." Culture is the heart of the organization, and its people are its pulse. A strong corporate culture isn't just measured in success – it's reflected in low absenteeism, high engagement, and a sense of being part of something greater.

When Lehman Brothers crashed in 2008, the world faced an economic storm. Many companies built shelters and tried to wait out the chaos. But those who truly succeeded? They built windmills and used the wind to generate energy.

It's the same with organizational culture. You can't predict all challenges, but you can build an organization that's agile, dynamic, and ready to act.

The Key Takeaway

Forget three-year plans and focus on creating results here and now. And remember – deficiencies in company culture can't be fixed with duct tape.

A culture built on values is also resilient. Whether it's about managing conflicts, making tough decisions, or navigating change, the culture will always lead the way. So next time you think about how to strengthen your organization, ask yourself: What is my good soil? And how can I make it even more fertile?

Summary

As a values-based leader, your task is to create an environment where both people and ideas can grow. It's about identifying the right people, using every opportunity to reinforce your values, and constantly reminding everyone of the deeper purpose. And most importantly – never losing sight of the culture because it defines everything else.

"People run companies, and values drive people. A strong culture creates strong results."

Leading with Trust and Confidence – The Art of Being Both Strong and Flexible

Think of nature. The palm tree that bends in Caribbean storms survives where oaks break. Water, soft and patient, wears down hard cliffs at the shoreline. Is that weakness? Hardly. Nature understands something many leaders forget – that strength often lies in flexibility.

A brilliant example of this is Angela Merkel, who during her time as Germany's Chancellor demonstrated this balance. When Europe faced the refugee crisis in 2015, Merkel decided to welcome hundreds of thousands of refugees. Despite enormous pressure both domestically and internationally, she stood firm in her values. She was strong in her convictions but flexible in her ability to negotiate and collaborate with other EU countries. It wasn't an easy decision, but her leadership showed that courage and trust in humanity's best can create lasting change.

Work Discipline – Build Momentum, Not Martyrdom

Work discipline isn't about showing how long you can stay in the office; it's about creating momentum that inspires others. Here are three ways to lead with discipline without burning out:

1. **Start with Clarity**
   Begin your day with a 10-minute plan of the three most important things you need to achieve. By prioritizing what creates the most value first, you become both productive and focused.

2. **Master Micro-Breaks**
   Take 5-10 minutes every couple of hours to reflect and gather your thoughts. It's not about working more but about working smarter with higher efficiency.

3. **Lead by Delivering**
   Your discipline isn't shown by how much you do but by the results you achieve. Let your actions speak louder than your presence.

An inspiring example is Marie Curie, who, despite enormous obstacles for women in science during her time, focused on what truly mattered – groundbreaking research. Her work with radioactivity, to which she dedicated her life, laid the foundation for significant medical advancements and earned Nobel Prizes in two different scientific fields.

By ignoring distractions and societal expectations, Curie focused on her purpose and demonstrated that perseverance and direction can lead to breakthroughs that change the world. Her work inspires us to prioritize what truly makes a difference.

Flexible Job Descriptions – From Rigid Routine to Dynamic Value Creation

Job descriptions don't have to be like outdated manuals gathering dust in a filing cabinet. Instead, they can be dynamic tools that create value and bring out the best in every employee. Here are three steps to create flexible job descriptions:

1. **Replace "Routine" with "Potential."**
   Instead of sticking to old tasks and processes, identify which activities create the most value for the team and the organization. Prioritize these and eliminate or automate those that simply waste time.
2. **Adapt Roles to Talents.**
   Stop forcing people into rigid job descriptions. View each individual as a unique resource and design roles that allow their strengths to shine. If someone excels at storytelling, give them a bigger role in communication. If someone is an expert at data, make them your analytical compass.
3. **Introduce Value-Creating Assignments.**
   Empower employees by giving them new, challenging tasks aligned with the company's vision and values. This not only motivates but also drives innovation and growth.

An example is Zappos, the American company known for its customer service. Zappos encourages its employees to push the boundaries of their roles to provide memorable and personal experiences for customers. One team at Zappos managed to arrange a customized solution for a customer by stepping outside standard routines and collaborating across departments. This flexibility and focus on customer needs have made Zappos a model of customer service excellence.

Meetings – Fewer, Shorter, Better (and with a Dose of Flexibility)

Meetings are often where creativity goes to die. But with the right mindset, they can become powerful tools for change and inspiration:
1. Reduce the number of meetings until people actually miss them (yes, it's possible).
2. **Make meeting formats flexible** – stand up, go outside, make them digital, or skip them entirely if they add no value.
3. **Always start meetings with a story or a concrete example tied to your values.**
   It's like kickstarting the meeting with a shot of strong espresso.

An inspiring example is Amazon's "two-pizza rule." Jeff Bezos, the company's founder, created a simple rule: no meeting should be so large that two pizzas can't feed everyone. This led to smaller, more effective meetings where everyone had a chance to contribute.

And here's the key question: What state do you want your meeting participants to leave the room in? Do you want them to feel inspired, forward-thinking, and proactive – or burdened and confused?

Here's a tip: Always end with a positive forward outlook. Highlight what has been achieved, clarify the next steps, and remind everyone why you're doing what you're doing. Replace "Any other business?" with "Today's successes" or "What do we take with us?" It creates energy and direction rather than draining it.

The Flexible Leadership – Flexibility as Strategy

And now we reach the core. Flexible leadership is your superpower. It's not about being weak or yielding but about being responsive, adaptable, and steadfast in your convictions.

1. **Stay strong by bending.**
   Think of palm trees in Caribbean storms. They bend but never break. Be like the palm tree – bend in the wind, strengthen your roots, and rise again.
2. **Challenge your own assumptions.**
   Look at the world from different perspectives. Think yin and yang – no up without down, no in without out. Dare to sit on the other side of the table and question your own beliefs. It doesn't make you weak – it makes you smart.
3. **Control your brain – and let your brain guide you.**
   As Carol Dweck says: Your brain is a muscle. Train it to think flexibly. Use it to build solutions, not barriers.
4. **See disagreements as opportunities.**
   J.K. Rowling faced twelve rejections before *Harry Potter* became a reality. She turned every setback into a lesson. What can you do with yours?

Summary: Lead Like a Master in Both Strength and Flexibility

Leading with trust and confidence doesn't mean being inflexible – it means balancing strength with adaptability. As a leader, you are both the rock and the water, the storm and the palm tree. You are the one who shows the way by listening, asking questions, and daring to rethink.

So next time you face a challenge, ask yourself:

- What can I bend without breaking?
- How can I strengthen the team through flexibility?
- Can we find a common path?

If you follow even half of this advice, I promise you'll unlock the door to leadership that inspires and lasts. The rest? You'll figure it out with a little humor and good coffee.

Chapter 4.

Motivating and Engaging the Team – The Art of Reviving a Stalled Cycle

"People will forget what you said, people will forget what you did, but people will never forget how you made them feel."
– Maya Angelou

According to a Gallup survey from 2023 – when everyone should understand that we're not just supposed to add our straw to the stack but carry entire logs – it turned out that only 13% of employees are motivated. On a 10-person bike, this means 1.3 people are pedaling forward, 6.3 are coasting, and 2.4 are braking. Yes, braking.

But let's be honest: the bike isn't going anywhere unless more people start pedaling. So, the question is: How do we get those who are braking to step off? How do we get those who are coasting to start pedaling? And how do we retain that one lone hero who's driving the team forward?

We start with a story – about a masterpiece that's been built over generations.

The Story of Sagrada Família and Its Builders

In the late 1800s, architect Antoni Gaudí began constructing the Sagrada Família in Barcelona, a cathedral that would become one of the world's most iconic buildings. But Gaudí knew from the beginning that he would never see his masterpiece completed. The cathedral was so grand and ambitious that it would take generations to finish.

Despite this, he assembled a team of builders and craftsmen who all had the same task: laying stones.

One day, during a tour of the construction site, a visitor asked three different workers what they were doing.

The first said, "I'm laying stones."

The second replied, "I'm building a wall."

But the third – he paused, looked up at the yet-unfinished towers, and smiled. "I'm building

Antoni Gaudí's cathedral, a symbol of our faith and Barcelona's pride. It will stand here for hundreds of years after I'm gone."

Three people. The same task. But only one understood the bigger purpose. Only one felt the pride of being part of something greater than themselves.

What do we learn from this? That motivation is about helping your employees understand why their work matters – that their "stones" are part of something much bigger.

Creating the Right Soil for Motivation

Motivated employees don't emerge out of thin air. They need the right environment – a place where they feel their work matters, where they grow, and where they can contribute. Here are three cornerstones:

1. **Freedom to Act and Influence**: No one wants a boss nitpicking every detail. When employees feel they have control over their work, their engagement grows.

2. **Development and Support**: Training, mentorship, and clear career paths aren't luxuries – they're investments in your company's future.

3. **A Meaningful Vision**: When people see how their work contributes to something greater – whether it's a "cathedral" or a new product – they're inspired to do their best.

The Seven Drivers of Motivation

So how do we motivate that bike team that's mostly coasting? Here are seven factors that can get the pedals moving:

1. **Fear** – Use sparingly. No one wants to lose their job, status, or future. Fear can motivate, but too much creates stress.
2. **Responsibility**: Give employees responsibility for something meaningful. When they see their decisions make a difference, pride and engagement grow.
3. **Gratitude**: Small words of appreciation can work wonders. Let your employees know why their work matters – and watch their motivation soar.
4. **Freedom**: Let people be creative. When they feel they can influence their work, it becomes more fun and meaningful.
5. **Belief in Success**: Paint a clear picture of hope for the future and show how each individual contributes to the journey.
6. **Achievement**: Set clear goals and make room to celebrate successes. Even small victories count.
7. **Revenge**: Challenge the team to prove their strength, to outdo themselves, and to show the world what they're capable of.

The 5 Hidden Motivation Killers

Want to know what will guarantee a drop in motivation? Here are 5 classic mistakes leaders make:

1. **Lack of Demands**: Nothing kills engagement faster than a boss who doesn't care about results. Without goals, there's no direction.
2. **Micromanagement**: Overly controlling leaders who obsess over every detail kill both creativity and engagement.
3. **Lack of Development**: When employees aren't allowed to grow, they'll soon look elsewhere.
4. **Unclear Goals**: If employees don't understand the company's objectives, how can they contribute?

5. **Lack of Recognition**: When achievements go unnoticed or unrewarded, motivation plummets. Feeling seen and appreciated is one of the strongest motivators.

The Secret of Value-Based Leadership

It's not about having a new ping-pong table or more team-building retreats. Motivation is about creating a culture where every employee feels seen, heard, and valued. That's the essence of value-based leadership.

So next time you see your team coasting, ask yourself:

- Do they have a cathedral to build?
- Do they understand why their work matters?
- Are they given the freedom and support they need to succeed?

The answer isn't in their hands. It lies in your leadership.

The Hockey Coach – The Art of Igniting a Team

"It's not the team with the best players that wins.
It's the team that plays best together."
– Herb Brooks

For the whole to work, the parts need to fit. This becomes glaringly obvious when you have five skaters and a goalie on the ice. If everyone doesn't do their job, the team loses. And what does it take for everyone to do their job? A clear game plan, laser focus, and ignition – three magical ingredients that every coach dreams of blending to perfection.

And who better to talk about ignition than Niklas Wikegård? A coach who understands that focus and fire go hand in hand. "Laser focus," as Wikegård puts it, isn't just about keeping an eye on the puck but knowing exactly what each player – or employee – should be doing.

But ignition isn't just the secret of hockey. It's a universal rule for all successful teams, whether they're chasing the Stanley Cup or budget goals. Let's dive into what it takes to spark the fire in your team.

The Story of "Notan" – Huddinge's Benchwarmer Who Conquered the NHL

Mattias Norström, or "Notan," is one of the most inspiring hockey players Sweden has produced. And ironically? He didn't even make the cut for Huddinge's junior team. But instead of giving up, he decided to become the best at what he could control: his fitness.

While others were out relaxing, Notan was looking for the nearest gym. On national team tours, he traveled with a weight belt, protein jars, and lifting shoes. He asked for the gym before even checking into the hotel. He had his focus, his routine – and he never hesitated.

The result? A career with the New York Rangers, Los Angeles Kings, and Dallas Stars. Half a billion kronor earned. How? By becoming an expert at what he could control.

What can we learn? If you know your strengths and weaknesses and work hard on what you can control, you can beat any opponent – on the rink or in the office.

Collect Ignition Fuel – Hannibal's Figs and Other Tricks

Did you know that Hannibal, the legendary warlord, fed his war elephants figs before battle? The figs irritated their skin, making the elephants so furious that they crushed everything in their path.

So the question is: What are your figs? What ignites you and your team?
- Is it negative news articles about your organization?
- Statements from competitors who underestimate you?

- Or perhaps a mantra like Churchill's "We shall never surrender"?

Whatever it is – use it. Find what sparks the fire in you and your team, and feed it until the glow becomes a blaze.

Build an Easy-to-Digest Mental Diet

The problem with many teams, both on the ice and at work, is that they try to do too much. But winners know that focus is the key. It's about boiling down the menu to just a few dishes. Here are some simple recipes for success:

1. **Be Specific.** If you don't know exactly what to focus on, how will you ignite? "Defend the goal at all costs" is easier to understand than "do a good job."

2. **Focus on a Few Things.** Narrow tasks down to a few key behaviors. Doing fewer things really well beats trying to do everything half-heartedly.

3. **Become an Expert in a Few Areas.** As Inge Hammarström, one of Sweden's best hockey players, used to say: "It's much better to be incredibly good at two things than mediocre at ten."

4. **Ignite with Pride.** True leaders make sure that every player – stars and benchwarmers alike – feels proud of their role.

Best When It Matters – Balancing Nervousness and Confidence

Niklas Lidström, perhaps the world's greatest defenseman of all time, admitted that he was nervous before every game. But he also knew how to use that nervousness to his advantage: short passes at the beginning, small successes that built confidence.

It's the same for your team. Help them start small and build success step by step. And remember: nervousness isn't the enemy – overexcitation is.

When Performance Is More Important Than Results

Hockey is the sport that measures everything: faceoffs, assists, goals. But sometimes it's dangerous to focus solely on the results. It's the same in the workplace. If you want each individual to give their best, provide feedback on effort – not just results.

The Coach's Summary on Ignition

1. Be specific.

2. Focus on a few things.

3. Be exceptionally good at a few areas.

4. Ignite with pride.

5. Know your strengths and weaknesses – the foundation for growth.

6. Collect ignition fuel – find your "figs."

7. Build confidence step by step.

And above all – don't forget to have fun! Because what's the point of winning if you're not enjoying the game?

Case Study:

According to neuroscientist Torkel Klingberg, there are different types of motivation: external motivation and internal motivation. External motivation occurs, for example, when children do their homework and are rewarded with an hour of gaming, or when we, as adults, go to work and receive a paycheck at the end of the month. Since Klingberg's research indicated that money doesn't have much to do with it, he turned his focus to internal motivation, which is the same as doing something simply because it feels right.

Klingberg describes an experiment where two groups were tasked with completing the same IQ exercise. One group was told that their results were due to their intelligence. The other group was praised for their effort. When both groups were given harder tasks to solve, those who were praised for their effort worked harder, while the "smarter" group was more likely to give up.

Chapter 5

Confidence and trust – the essence of values-based leadership

Introduction:

Confidence and trust are the fundamental building blocks of successful and value-based leadership. But let's be honest – it's not always easy. We've all encountered leaders who grasp control like a lifeline, never quite daring to let go. But what if we could lead like water instead? Adaptable, durable and strong. Water always finds a way.

1. Lead like water – adaptability and strength
"That which is soft, adaptable and enduring overcomes all obstacles in time."

Water is the best metaphor for leadership. It is flexible enough to adapt to any container, but also powerful enough to shape landscapes. So what can we learn from water? Here are three keys to fluid leadership:

- **Don't grip too hard:** If you try to control everything and everyone, you lose both trust and team commitment. Open up, let go and let the team flow within the right framework.

- **Let it flow:** Stagnant water becomes diseased – and the same goes for stagnant organizations. Put frames that control the flow without throttling it.

- **Do not place yourself above others:** Water always seeks the lowest point, where it gathers strength and creates depth. Be humble as a leader, listen more than you speak and strengthen your team from the ground up.

Maria, 29 years old, is the founder and CEO of SoftFlow, a tech startup in Malmö that develops cloud-based solutions for small businesses. The company has been in existence for two years and has already attracted five talented employees with high ambitions. As an important project for a new client, a retail chain, approaches the deadline, Maria feels the pressure. Customers have high expectations and the team works hard to deliver.

Maria is faced with a choice: to control every detail herself or to trust her team. She realizes that if she tries to control everything, she will drain both herself and the team. Instead, she chooses to give the team the freedom to make their own decisions within clearly defined goals and frameworks. She tells them: "I believe in you and your ideas. Do what you think is best to solve the challenges."

The result? Not only is the project delivered on time, it also exceeds the client's expectations. The team presents a creative solution that impresses greatly. Reflecting on the success, Maria says, "When I let go of control, I saw the team flourish. Their confidence grew, and we found new ways to work together."

SoftFlow's journey during this time shows that leadership, like water, is about creating room for growth. By trusting her team, Maria not only built trust, but also a stronger company culture.

2. Build Trust Through Actions and Values

Trust starts with you as a leader. It's about living by the values you preach and showing that you are reliable in both words and actions. People don't follow what you say—they follow what you do. Therefore, it is crucial to:

- **Show Integrity:** Always keep your promises, whether they are big or small.
- **Communicate Honestly:** Be clear and transparent, even when the messages are hard to convey.
- **Model Behaviors:** Show what is acceptable through your own actions. This sets the standard for the whole team.

Practical example: Imagine a situation where a tough deadline must be met. Instead of delegating the entire responsibility, show that you are willing to work alongside the team to complete the task. This creates a „we" feeling and strengthens trust.

3. Trust Through Motivation and Responsibility

Delegating responsibility is one of the most powerful ways to build trust. When you show that you trust the team's ability to make decisions and do their work, a positive cycle of engagement and self-confidence is created. Here are some keys to achieving this:

- **Set Clear Expectations:** Clarify what is expected and then allow space for the team to deliver.
- **Celebrate Successes:** Acknowledge and reward efforts that contribute to goals. Small successes lead to greater achievements.
- **Give Feedback**: Positive feedback builds motivation, and targeted feedback helps develop skills.

Practical example: Let an employee lead a project with greater responsibility than before. Provide support when needed, but allow them to make their own decisions. When they succeed, reinforce the success by publicly acknowledging their achievement.

4. Create a Culture of Trust and Inclusion

Trust is not only built between leaders and employees—it must also exist among team members. An inclusive and trustworthy culture is one that:

- **Encourages Openness**: Create an environment where it is safe to share ideas and thoughts without fear of judgment.
- **Promotes Collaboration**: Strengthen the team spirit through shared goals and activities.
- **Handles Mistakes Constructively**: Use mistakes as learning opportunities rather than reasons for criticism.

Practical example: Implement regular reflection meetings where the team can discuss what has worked well and what can be improved. This creates a habit of openness and improvement. Make sure to conclude the meeting on a positive and hopeful note.

Summary: How to Create a Mentality and Lead Like Water

1. **Build a Shared Vision**: Everyone must play the same game and strive toward the same goal.

2. **Delegate Clearly**: Give responsibility and freedom, but without abdicating your own responsibility.

3. **Provide Flexible Boundaries**: They should be clear enough to create focus but flexible enough for creativity.

4. **Empower the Team**: Provide tools and authority to act, and trust that they will do the right thing.

5. **Lead Like Water**: Adapt, flow forward, and empower the team with humility.

6. **Celebrate and Learn from Results**: Acknowledge successes but also reflect on what can be improved.

7. **Create a Culture of Responsibility**: Collaboration and accountability are not optional – they are the key to success.

Conclusion: Trust is not something built overnight, but through consistent effort, it can become the foundation for successful leadership. When you, as a leader, show that you trust your team, live according to your values, and create an inclusive culture, you lay the foundation for both individual and organizational success. Ask yourself: How can I show my team every day that they are valued and trusted?

Summary of Part 2: Leading Others

The Essence of Leadership Leading others means creating an environment where people grow, collaborate, and feel a deep connection to the organization's purpose. By building trust, inspiring, and empowering the team, you don't just shape results – you shape individuals who dare to dream bigger and perform better. Part 2 takes us from theories of control to value-driven leadership, where trust and responsibility are at the center.

Keys to Successful Leadership:

1. **The Power of Coaching**: Build self-confidence, create clarity, and help employees unlock their potential. It's a journey that begins with listening and curiosity.
2. **Communication and Conflict Management**: Conflicts are an opportunity to build stronger relationships. Learn to listen with empathy and communicate with clarity to turn challenges into opportunities.
3. **Team Development and Culture**: The soul of the organization is its culture – create a fertile ground where both people and ideas can grow. Highlight values and create unity through shared goals.
4. **Motivation and Engagement**: Motivated team members drive the entire organization forward. Build freedom, offer appreciation, and show why their work matters.
5. **The Power of Trust**: Trust is the foundation. Let go of control, trust the team, and let them take responsibility for their success.

As Lao Tzu said: the best leader is the one who is barely noticed, where the team proudly says, "That? We did that!" It's leadership that builds not just results, but also confidence, culture, and long-term sustainability.

Conclusion: Leadership is about daring to let go, creating direction, and empowering others to reach their best selves. Build your leadership style on values, listening, and a strong belief in people's potential. It's not just a path to strong results – it's a path to a better world.

Reflection Questions for Leading Others:

1. How can you adapt your leadership to create an environment where people dare to grow and take responsibility?
2. What changes in your communication and conflict management could strengthen relationships within your team?
3. How are your values reflected in the culture you are building and developing in the workplace?
4. How do you motivate your team to see the bigger purpose behind their work? What can you do to reinforce their engagement?
5. How can you build trust by being more flexible while still holding onto clear goals?

Part 3: Leading the Organization

Introduction

Leading a business is like being the captain of a ship in a constantly changing sea. There are days with calm waters and sunshine – and then there are days with storms, high waves, and a crew that wants to go in different directions. Your role as a leader is to stay on course, even when the weather conditions are far from perfect. And if we're being honest: it's in the storm that you show what you're truly made of.

Running a business is dancing between short-term wins and long-term goals, between the cheers of success and the criticism that sneaks in when things go wrong. You need to be able to stand in the middle of this chaos and still hold on to the values that make your business unique. As Lao Tzu beautifully reminds us: "The one who dares to be vulnerable is the strongest of all." Leading with humility is not a weakness – it's a superpower.

But let's not forget the most important thing: leadership can also be fun. It's not just about solving problems or reading reports – it's about creating something meaningful, helping others grow, and building a culture where people are proud to contribute. Humor and warmth are not just the spice in leadership – they are part of the recipe for success.

So, how do you become the leader who not only stays on course in fair winds but also finds the strength to sail straight through the storms? It starts with you – your vision, your values, and your courage to both hold on and let go when necessary. But above all, it's about daring to be human in a world that often focuses on performance and results.

As a business leader, you have the opportunity to create something bigger than yourself – a culture where every person feels important, every decision has meaning, and every step brings you closer to a sustainable future.

When you lead with balance and humility, you create not only a successful business but also leave a legacy that inspires others to continue the journey long after you've docked.

So, what are you waiting for? It's time to take the helm and create a business that doesn't just survive but makes a difference. The future starts here – with you.

Table of content

Chapter 1: Strategies for Organizational Management

Creating clear and effective strategies is the foundation for leading a business or organization. A strategy differs from tactics in that it is the long-term vision that points out the direction. Tactics involve the daily actions that support the strategy. Sun Tzu says it best: "Strategy without tactics is the slowest route to victory. Tactics without strategy are the noise before defeat."
Focus:
- Define strategy and tactics: Understand their roles and how they interact.
- Strategic goals: How they give direction and inspire.
- Case studies: Volvo's focus on safety and Telia's simplicity.

Strategies are stable, but they must be supported by tactical actions that deliver results here and now. It's about creating a map and equipping the team with the tools to follow it.

Chapter 2: Agile and Dynamic Leadership

In today's fast-moving world, leadership must be flexible and adaptable. Dynamic leadership is about juggling multiple factors simultaneously and adjusting the course as needed. Agile leadership is based on learning and the ability to quickly react to new conditions.
Focus:

- Flexibility: Embrace change as an opportunity.
- The role of the team: Create a culture where employees take responsibility and adapt.
- Examples: Denver Airport's "storm workshops" and a restaurant's agile methods.

By implementing agile methods, leaders can create an organization that not only reacts to changes but also leads them.

Chapter 3: Growth-Oriented Leadership

Growth is about daring to take initiative, drive innovation, and challenge the status quo. It starts with identifying and removing obstacles that hinder development.
Focus:

- Identify obstacles: What stands in the way of growth?
- Innovation: Create new opportunities through creativity and courage.
- Examples: LEGO's turnaround and NASA's handling of limitations during the Apollo program.

Growth is not just economic success – it's about creating movement forward, inspiring the team, and building an organization that can meet future challenges.

Chapter 4: Parallel and Delegative Leadership

Parallel leadership involves managing multiple processes at once without losing direction. Together with effective delegation, this ensures that resources are used optimally and the team stays engaged.
Focus:

- Manage complexity: Create structure for multiple simultaneous processes.
- Delegation: Give freedom and responsibility to the team without losing control.
- Examples: Tesla's production strategies and IKEA's success with flat-pack furniture.

A leader who can balance between being involved and delegating builds a culture of trust and efficiency.

Chapter 5: Goal Management and Follow-up

Without clear goals, work becomes aimless and inefficient. Goal management is about creating direction, while follow-up ensures that efforts lead to the desired results.
Focus:

- The RAC model: Results, Activity, and Competence as a foundation.
- Examples: Netflix's transformation and Amazon's customer focus.
- Tools: How leaders can measure progress and adapt strategies.

Goal management is not just a method – it's a mindset that creates clarity, focus, and engagement.

Chapter 6: Crisis Management ABC

Crisis management is one of the greatest challenges a leader can face. By acting quickly and strategically, you can turn a crisis into an opportunity.
Focus:

1. **Airbreathing** – Create calm and clarity:
   - Take control of the situation and communicate clearly.
   - Structure actions using the model Facts – Explanation – Action.
   - Example: A Swedish sports chain's handling of criticism about working conditions.
2. **Bleeding** – Manage time and arguments under pressure:
   - Acknowledge mistakes quickly and show decisiveness.
   - Example: A Swedish bank's open handling of a data breach.
3. **Crash** – Act with courage:

- Navigate through the different phases of a crisis with the model Then–Now–Since.
- Example: SAS's handling of the ash cloud in 2010 and the Tylenol poisoning cases.

Examples and lessons:
- SAS: How clear communication and actions won customer trust.
- NASA: Successful delegation and collaboration during the Apollo program.
- Johnson & Johnson: Handling the Tylenol crisis as an example of value-based leadership.

Summary: Crisis management is about combining courage, clarity, and speed. Value-based leadership creates stability under pressure and sees crises as opportunities to build trust and long-term strength.

Chapter 7: Mental Strategies and Decision-Making

Mental strategies and decision-making are central skills for successful leadership. They help leaders navigate complexity, make wise decisions, and maintain focus.
Focus:

1. The Chinese Farmer: The story of how perspective and mental attitude influence the ability to handle setbacks and see opportunities.
2. Henry Ford's Determination: How courage and focus led to groundbreaking success in the automotive industry.
3. Three principles for mental strategies:
   - Prioritize one path over many.
   - Put the whole before the details.
   - Keep the goal in sight, but be flexible in handling challenges.
4. Reflections for leaders: Questions that help identify strengths, prioritize goals, and make better decisions.

Examples:

- Leonardo da Vinci's strategic thinking and long-term focus.
- Practical tips such as avoiding indecision and using pros and cons lists.

Summary: Developing mental strategies is about daring to make decisions and taking control of your focus. As the Roman philosopher Seneca said, "Happiness is what happens when preparation meets opportunity." By prioritizing and thinking long-term, leaders build a sustainable foundation for success.

For Leaders – What is it Really About?

Anxiety, endless meetings, and documentation have become everyday life for many leaders. It's as if we've lost sight of the core of leadership – creating action forward. Doing things the "right way" seems to have become more important than doing the right things. And you know what? The world outside isn't waiting for the perfect meeting notes.

Patrik Hall, a professor of political science at Malmö University, points to a development where bureaucracy risks suffocating results. Organizations build staffs instead of value, administer instead of acting, and chase titles instead of achievements. Meanwhile, the world outside is rushing forward with tougher competition, reduced margins, and rapid AI development.

Do you recognize these symptoms?

- „I don't have time."
- "We don't have enough time."
- "It's not within my area of responsibility."
- „We need more resources."
- "We need a meeting for this!"

At the same time, groups gather to discuss pseudo-problems, while the real potential of the team is stifled by waiting for perfect consensus. But being a leader is about something else – something more authentic and valuable.

Value-Based Leadership – The Core of Success

Leadership is not just a title or a line on your CV. It's about creating real value through other people. And value-based leadership means:

- Lifting people to new heights through an inspiring work environment.
- Daring to prioritize what really matters – and communicating that.
- Being consistent in follow-ups and standing firm in your direction.
- Not avoiding difficult decisions but facing them, with your head held high and being present.

It's not always comfortable. It's not always smooth. But leadership is about stepping forward, daring to make decisions even when it's tough, and understanding that success is not measured by the number of meetings, but by the difference you make for your employees and your organization.

So, next time someone says "We need a meeting for this," ask instead: "What can we do right now to create action?" Because that's exactly what leadership is about – creating action and bringing us closer to the goals that truly matter.

Chapter 1.

Strategies for Business Management

Strategic Definitions – The Key to Success

How often have you heard the words "strategy" and "tactics" thrown around in leadership groups as if they were synonyms? To be honest, few can really explain the difference – perhaps because we often let them blend together like coffee and milk. But understanding their unique roles is like having the right map and compass in unfamiliar terrain. It's crucial not just for navigating the business, but also for inspiring and engaging employees and customers.

Telia is a classic example. When they transformed from Televerket in 1993, they set "simplicity" as their guiding star. "It should be as easy to do business with us as it is to turn on a lightbulb," was their mantra. Sounds smart, right? But here's the question: Is simplicity a strategy or a tactical principle?

What Are Strategy and Tactics – Really?

A strategy is your starry sky, the direction that points toward future goals. It is stable, long-term, and driven by values rather than trends. Tactics, on the other hand, are your toolbox – the short-term actions and tricks that move you forward right now. Strategy is "what" and "why," while tactics are "how" and "when." Both are essential, but they serve entirely different functions.

Let's take Volvo as an example. Their strategy has been the same since 1927: safety. It doesn't matter if they're producing in Torslanda or Shanghai, whether it's a booming economy or a financial crisis – safety is always top priority.

The strategy does not change because of temporary external factors – it is stable and guiding, no matter where you are geographically or market-wise.

Tactically, however, it may involve different solutions depending on the market or technology.

Strategy and Tactics – The Symbiosis

But here's the interesting part: strategy and tactics cannot live without each other. They are like yin and yang. The strategy sets the direction, but without tactical actions, it's just a vision on paper. Tactics deliver results, but without strategy, it's just a noise of activities without context. This is where we need the "stratactical" – a collaboration where strategic goals and tactical actions are woven together to create real value.

Think of sustainability, quality, or health. These can be used both strategically and tactically depending on the context. They become hybrids that drive both long-term goals and operational results.

Sun Tzu Said It Best

The Chinese general Sun Tzu nailed it more than 2500 years ago:

> *"Strategy without tactics is the slow path to victory.*
> *Tactics without strategy are just the noise before defeat."*

And isn't that the truth? To build a value-based leadership that withstands change and the future, we need to understand and respect this balance. When we clarify the roles between strategy and tactics, we don't just get a clearer map – we gain the power to lead the business forward with courage, humor, and care.

So, the next time you wonder whether you need a strategy or tactics, pause and ask yourself: "Does this **create long-term value**, or is it just solving today's problems?" That's where **you'll find the answer.**

Chapter 2.

Agile and dynamic leadership

The dynamic leadership – a force for action

Dynamic leadership – a force for action

Dynamic leadership is like juggling on a unicycle – you have to keep everything in motion while constantly balancing to avoid crashing. It's about generating energy and direction, making sure the team moves forward towards the goals without spinning in circles. And yes, it also means that sometimes you need to slow down a bit, or else you risk accelerating straight into a ditch.

But remember: it's not about throwing money and resources at every problem. In fact, too many resources can kill creativity, much like serving a gourmet meal every day – no one will appreciate the taste anymore. Success is born from focus, not abundance.

Denver Airport and the Storm Chaos

Denver International Airport is known for its winter storms, where snow chaos often halts traffic and places thousands of passengers on waiting lists. In 2019, the airport's manager, Ahmed, faced one of the worst snowstorms in years. The standard protocols – long meetings, bureaucratic processes, and time-consuming decision chains – had previously proven insufficient to handle the chaos.

Ahmed realized that something needed to change. He introduced a new way of working: "storm workshops." When a weather warning came, he quickly gathered all involved teams – from ground staff to air traffic controllers – in a crisis center. Instead of following old manuals, they focused on creating quick, real-time solutions. Everyone contributed, regardless of hierarchy.

During the first storm with this new setup, the airport reduced delays by 40% and kept two critical flights on time – something that had previously been considered impossible. The team described it as a "storm dance," where everyone moved in sync. Denver demonstrated how dynamic leadership doesn't just solve problems – it builds pride and trust among all involved.

Agile Leadership – Learning, Flexibility, and Success

Agile leadership is a bit like being a hockey coach during a storm match – you may have a plan, but you have to be ready to adjust it at all times. It's about understanding the game, seeing what's happening in real-time, and coaching the team to do its best under the prevailing conditions.

But agile leadership is not for those who love to maintain control. Here, you create the right conditions, give clear goals, and then step aside. It's not your job to skate with the puck – your job is to create the plan where the team can play its best game. And if you think you always have all the answers, let's be honest: you don't. Agile leadership is about exploring, adapting, and learning along the way.

The Restaurant in Austin That Found Its Flow

In the heart of Austin, Texas, Sophie opened a new restaurant known for its creative Tex-Mex dishes. But success quickly became a problem. Guests were flooding in faster than the kitchen could handle, and tension between the chefs and waitstaff grew. Complaints started popping up on Yelp, and Sophie realized she risked losing her spark – and her customers.

She decided to implement an agile approach in the kitchen. She put up a large sign that read: "A perfect kitchen is a kitchen in motion." Every evening began with a brief planning session where chefs and waitstaff discussed the night's goals, expected rush times, and potential challenges. After each shift, they held a five-minute feedback round, where everyone shared what worked and what needed to be adjusted.

Two weeks later, the change began to show. Dishes went out faster, servers had better communication with the kitchen, and customer reviews on Yelp went from three to five stars. Sophie realized that agile leadership is about creating an environment where the team can grow together, whether running a business or a restaurant in Austin.

The Mental Movement of Leadership

In the end, dynamic and agile leadership is about creating both energy and direction. It's about juggling and balancing, keeping the movement going, and daring to change course when necessary. It's about creating action – and doing it with a smile on your face.

So the next time you feel like everything is chaos, ask yourself: "Are we maintaining balance, or is it time to adjust the course?" And if you want to keep the team on the right path, maybe it's time to get inspired by Denver's storm workshop or the restaurant's feedback round in Austin. Sometimes, the unexpected is exactly what's needed to create the dynamic that moves you forward.

Chapter 3

Growth-oriented leadership

Growth-oriented leadership – Choosing to lead, not follow

Growth always begins with a choice.

Do you dare to take the lead, challenge the familiar, and bet on the future, or do you stay in the comfort zone and settle for following? In a world where AI, globalization, and technological innovations drive change faster than we can blink, that choice is crucial.

Growth is no longer a luxury, it's a survival strategy.
    The big question is: **How do you lead growth when the playing field is constantly changing**?

Step One: Passivate anti-development forces

Every organization has them – those who slow down development. They can take the form of ingrained structures, long meetings without results, or people who resist change. These forces are subtle but deadly, and to drive growth, you need to identify them and take action.
    An effective way to do this is by analyzing all parts of the organization and asking a few simple but powerful questions:

- Does this create customer value?
- Does it contribute to increased revenue?
- Does it reduce costs?
- Does it help mitigate risks?
- Does it support the organization's long-term strategy?

If something doesn't contribute to these goals, it's time to question why it exists. This process may feel brutal, but it not only creates clarity but also space for innovation and progress.

LEGO and the Dramatic Turnaround

Let's talk about LEGO, one of the world's most beloved brands. In the early 2000s, the company was on the verge of bankruptcy. They had lost their focus and spread their resources over too many areas, from video games to theme parks. Customers no longer recognized the brand, and the company's core product – the building blocks – had become a secondary concern.

When Jørgen Vig Knudstorp took over as CEO in 2004, he took the first step in growth-oriented leadership: he identified and eliminated everything that didn't create value for customers. Theme parks were sold, unprofitable product lines were discontinued, and focus was returned to the company's core – creative building blocks.

The result? LEGO went from near collapse to becoming the world's most profitable toy company. By passive development-resistant forces, regaining control over its values, and prioritizing customer needs, LEGO became a shining example of growth-oriented leadership.

Step Two: Create Success Through Limitations

Sometimes, the key to success is not more resources but fewer. Limitations can be the catalyst that drives sharpness, creativity, and innovation. When resources are limitless, there's no need to think outside the box, but when they're limited, every decision becomes crucial.

NASA and the Moon Landing

In 1961, the USA faced an enormous challenge. The Soviet Union had just sent the first human into space, and the pressure on NASA was immense. President Kennedy set a goal: to land a man on the moon and bring him back safely – within a decade.

But NASA faced enormous limitations: the budget was tight, the technology didn't exist, and no one even had a manual for how a moon landing should take place. It was these very limitations that became their greatest asset. Engineers were forced to think in new ways, optimize every gram in the spacecraft, and develop solutions never seen before.

On July 20, 1969, Apollo 11 landed on the moon, and humanity took one of its greatest steps forward – all thanks to innovation born from the pressure of limitations.

Step Three: Dynamic Perspectives Create Momentum

Growth is not just about courage and focus – it's about creating movement. A value-based leadership sees opportunities where others see obstacles. It dares to embrace uncertainty and uses creativity as its primary fuel.

Spotify and the Revolution of the Music Industry

In the early 2000s, the music industry was facing an existential crisis. Piracy had taken over, and record labels were struggling to survive. Then came two Swedish entrepreneurs, Daniel Ek and Martin Lorentzon, with an idea that would change everything. They asked themselves: "What if we could offer all the world's music – legally – for a small monthly fee?"

Their idea was as simple as it was revolutionary, but the road to success was anything but easy. They faced stiff opposition from record labels, technical challenges, and a skeptical market. But by sticking to their vision and adapting along the way, they built Spotify – a platform that today is an integral part of our daily lives.

Spotify showed the world that dynamic and value-based leadership can change an entire industry – and create growth in a time of uncertainty.

Growth Starts and Ends with Leadership

Whether you run an iconic toy company, send people to the moon, or revolutionize how we listen to music, growth is about the same core principles:

- Eliminate barriers and obstacles.
- Use limitations as a catalyst for creativity.
- Create movement through dynamic and creative perspectives.

Growth is not a straight path. It is full of obstacles, resistance, and uncertainty. But for those who dare to take the lead, there is also an opportunity to create something that leaves a mark far beyond today's goals.

The question is: Do you dare to lead growth, or will you choose to stay in the comfortable? For those who wait – also wait to be overtaken.

Chapter 4.

Parallel, delegating and uncompromising leadership

Being a Leader Today is Like Juggling Oranges, Balls, and a Chainsaw at the Same Time – While Riding a Bicycle Uphill.

It's about having full control, even when the circumstances are chaotic. The world we live and lead in requires not just multitasking but also the ability to delegate correctly and dare to be uncompromising when necessary. We must be both the captain steering the ship, the orchestra conductor setting the tempo, and the commander making tough decisions without hesitation.

The Traps of Series Connection

Many leaders still get stuck in the old model of series connection: "We'll take one problem at a time, finish project X before even looking at project Y." It sounds wise, but in practice, it often leads to meeting inflation, procrastination, and fear of making mistakes. Professor Patrik Hall warns against this – a work culture where processes and bureaucracy stand in the way of results.

But in today's fast-moving reality, we simply can't afford this type of sluggishness. Succeeding as a leader is about creating movement, building trust, and making clear decisions – in parallel.

The Future of Parallel Leadership

Imagine a supermarket manager. While the milk is running out on the shelves, campaigns need to be rolled out, checkout lines handled, and the cooling system serviced – all while someone in the HR department calls in sick. To succeed in such chaos requires multitasking, clear priorities, and a sharp ability to delegate.

Parallel leadership is the art of managing several processes simultaneously – without drowning in them. It's about giving your employees enough freedom to act while keeping control of the bigger picture.

Apollo 13

When the Apollo 13 mission to the moon faced a catastrophic explosion in space in 1970, all hope seemed lost. With limited resources and time working against them, the team on Earth and the crew onboard had to think quickly and creatively to solve an impossible problem: bringing the astronauts back safely.

By focusing on solutions instead of obstacles and using everything they had available in an innovative way, a potential tragedy was turned into one of space exploration's most celebrated rescue operations.

The lesson? Success is not about avoiding problems but solving them with focus, creativity, and collaboration.

Uncompromising Leadership – When Clarity is the Key

Parallel working and delegation only work when the leader has the courage to be uncompromising when necessary. Being uncompromising isn't about being harsh for the sake of it, but about standing firm on what is right, even when it's uncomfortable.

Mary Barra and the Transformation of General Motors

When Mary Barra took over as CEO of General Motors, the company was facing a massive crisis. Faulty ignition switches had been linked to several deaths, and the company was in a deep economic slump. Barra chose to act quickly and uncompromisingly: she initiated a comprehensive internal review and fired several senior executives who hadn't delivered. She followed this with a global recall of millions of vehicles, a move that cost billions but showed customers that GM was taking responsibility.

At the same time, she shifted the company's strategy toward the future, focusing on electric vehicles and autonomous technology. Under her leadership, GM has not only regained customer trust but also become a leader in innovation.

This is a brilliant example of how uncompromising leadership can turn a crisis into an opportunity.

Keys to Parallel, Delegating, and Uncompromising Leadership

1. **Clear Goals**
   If you don't know where you're going, it doesn't matter what decisions you make. Value-based leadership is built on clear and precise goals that show the team what's most important. Goals act as a map – without them, everyone fumbles in the dark.

2. **Change Readiness**
   Change is not a threat – it's an opportunity. A parallel leader knows when it's time to change strategies and embraces uncertainty as a natural part of the process.

3. **The Right Conditions**
   Delegation is not about throwing tasks over the fence and hoping for the best. It requires clarity, resources, and authority. Give your teams what they need to succeed.

4. **Solution-Focused**
   Problems are just disguised opportunities. Having a solution-focused mindset helps you see obstacles as steps toward success. Act quickly, learn from mistakes, and adjust course.

5. **Courage to Make Tough Decisions**
   Uncompromising leadership requires courage. You must dare to make decisions that may not be popular, but are right for the long-term success of the organization.

Turning On and Turning Off

Successful parallel and delegating leadership requires knowing when to accelerate and when to slow down. Here are a few rules of thumb:

Turn On:

- **Optimism:** See the opportunities, not just the problems.
- **Focus on Value:** Prioritize what really matters.
- **Flexibility:** Be ready to change course when necessary.

Turn Off:

- **Procrastination:** Don't wait for perfect conditions – act now.
- **Negativity:** Don't let obstacles drain your energy.
- **Guilt:** You can't do everything. And that's okay.

Conclusion: The Art of Juggling Leadership

Parallel, delegating, and uncompromising leadership isn't about multitasking in the traditional sense. It's the art of prioritizing, delegating, and creating a culture where every individual feels supported and inspired. When you, as a leader, can juggle oranges, balls, and a chainsaw without losing the rhythm – then you're not just a leader. You're an inspiration.

So next time chaos knocks, ask yourself: "What can I delegate? What can I prioritize? And how can I create movement forward?" The answer may not always be obvious, but that's where the journey begins.

Chapter 5.

Goal management and follow-up – With RAC as the basis for success

Leadership Without Goals is Like Trying to Navigate a Ship Without a Compass.

It might feel like you're making progress, but in reality, you're just drifting. To create direction, drive, and results, you need a clear method – and that's where the RAK model comes into play.

RAC – Results, Activity, and Competence – is not just three letters. It's a mindset that helps you prioritize, lead, and follow up in a way that creates real change. It's simple enough for a rookie to grasp, yet powerful enough to turn around an entire organization. So, let's dive in!

What is RAC?

1. **R – Results: Setting the Sights**
   Results are not about chasing numbers for the sake of numbers. It's about setting clear, meaningful, and measurable goals. Ask yourself: What is it we actually want to achieve? It can be anything from increased revenue to more satisfied customers or larger market shares. But let's be honest – results aren't just a milestone. They are a signal showing whether your activities are actually leading you in the right direction. Spend 20% of your time reflecting on what has been, and 80% planning ahead. Results act as a compass, keeping you and your team on course.

Example: Imagine a relay team. The goal is to win the race. The result is the final position, but to get there, the team must analyze each runner's performance, evaluate the handoffs, and adjust tactics. It's about working smarter, not just harder.

2. **A – Activities: Doing the Job Right**
   Results are never achieved without the right activities. This is the engine in RAK. Ask yourself three simple questions:
   - **Focus:** Which activities drive the most value? Customer meetings? Product development? Marketing?
   - **Frequency:** How often should activities be carried out to create momentum?
   - **Quality:** How do we ensure we're doing the right things in the right way?

A successful leader always identifies the most important activity (VA) – the one that has the biggest impact on the goal. It's about not spreading yourself and the team too thin. Think of a laser beam: if the light spreads too much, it becomes weak, but if it's focused, it can cut through steel.

Metaphor: A farmer can't plant the entire field at once. But if he focuses on planting in the best soil and waters regularly, he'll harvest more than anyone else.

3. **C – Competence: The Key to Sustainable Results**
   Competence is the foundation on which everything rests. Without the right knowledge and skills, even the best strategies risk falling flat. This is about building a team that is constantly developing. Competence is not a luxury – it's a necessity.
   Build competence on three levels:
- **Experience:** Learn from past successes and mistakes.
- **Theory:** Keep the team updated with the latest insights and trends.
- **Engagement:** Inspire employees to grow both as individuals and as part of the organization.

Remember Netflix. When they realized their future didn't lie in DVD rentals but in streaming, they invested heavily in building competence in technology and customer behavior. By setting a clear goal – to become the global leader in entertainment – and shifting focus to activities that supported that goal, they revolutionized an entire industry. At the same time, they invested in creating an organization where innovation and learning were central.

RAC in Practice – How to Apply the Model

1. **Start with the result:** Set a goal that is measurable, challenging, and inspiring. Think big but concrete. What do you want to achieve in the next six months?
2. **Define the activities:** What efforts will drive you toward the goal? Identify and prioritize what makes the biggest difference. Put all your energy there and dare to say no to distractions.
3. **Invest in competence:** What does the team need to learn to succeed? Create a culture where continuous learning is the norm.
4. **Follow up and adjust:** Use regular check-ins to ensure you're on the right track. Don't be afraid to adjust goals or activities if new insights arise.

The Seven Questions of Goal Setting – The Key to Clarity

Setting goals is not just about knowing what you want. It's about answering the seven questions that build a stable foundation for success: What, Who, Why, Where, When, How, and With What help. Here's a quick guide:

1. **What:** What do you want to achieve? Be clear and specific. A clearly defined goal works like a GPS.
2. **Who:** Who should be involved? The right people in the right places are crucial.
3. **Why:** Why is this goal important? A strong "why" creates engagement.
4. **Where:** Where should it happen? Identify the area where the change is needed.
5. **When:** What is the timeline? A goal without a deadline is just a dream.
6. **How:** What is the strategy? Clear steps create clear direction.
7. **With What help:** What resources do you need? This can range from technology to skill development.

Reflection

Imagine you are in the kitchen, preparing to bake a cake. In front of you are all the ingredients, but no recipe to follow. What happens then? Likely a mess – that might taste okay, but could also fail completely. RAC is like your leadership recipe: it shows you step by step how to build a successful organization – just like following a recipe to create a perfect cake.

To truly benefit from RAC, stop and ask yourself these questions:

- What is my most important result goal right now?
- What few activities should I prioritize to reach it?
- What competence do I and my team need to develop to succeed?

Write down your answers and use them as a compass to start acting today.

Conclusion: RAC is more than a model – it's a mindset

Working with goal management is not about doing more, but about doing the right things. With RAC, you focus on what really matters – results, activities, and competence – and build an organization that not only survives but thrives. The question is not whether you can succeed, but what you can achieve when you use the right focus.

So next time results aren't coming in, ask yourself:

- Do we have a clear goal?
- Are we focusing on the right things?
- Do we have the right competence?

And remember: RAC is your compass. Aim forward, fuel with energy, and take every step with courage and determination!

Chapter 6.

The ABCs of crisis management – Acting with courage and value-based leadership

Airbreathing – Bleeding – Crash.

Crisis Management – The First Aid of Leadership

Just like in first aid, where actions are taken to stabilize and minimize damage until expert help arrives, the same principles apply in crisis management. It's about creating clarity, stopping bleeding, and handling shock – with speed and precision. With the right strategy, you can turn a crisis into an opportunity.

1. Airbreathing – Create Clarity and Control

When the crisis strikes, it's easy to fall into panic mode. But as a leader, your first task is to take a deep breath and create calm. Panic is contagious – but calm is, too.

- **Take control of the situation:** What do we know? What is the most important thing right now?
- **Reason forward:** Structure arguments and actions in three steps:
  - **Facts:** What happened?
  - **Explanation:** Why did it happen?
  - **Action:** What are we doing next?
- **Build a clear communication plan** that gives the team a sense of direction and security.

Example:
When a European sports chain faced criticism for poor working conditions in its factories, the leadership quickly gathered facts and communicated openly:

- What happened? Inspections missed irregularities.
- Why? They lacked the resources to follow up adequately.
- What are we doing? They immediately implemented independent third-party audits and strengthened follow-up procedures.

Result: A crisis that could have damaged their reputation turned into an opportunity to demonstrate decisiveness and a willingness to improve.

2. Bleeding – Managing Time and Arguments Under Pressure

When time is short and the pressure is high, it's easy to fall into a defensive position. But shifting the blame always weakens your position. This requires courage and clear strategies.

A. Acknowledgment as a Weapon

A quick and honest acknowledgment can build trust. Provide rational explanations:

1. **Lack of knowledge:** "We didn't have all the information at the time."
2. **Lack of insight:** "We didn't fully understand the consequences."
3. **Lack of resources:** "We didn't have the right tools."

Example:
When a well-known Swedish bank was hit by a data breach, the leadership chose to acknowledge the issues immediately:
- "We didn't have sufficient security systems in place, and that was a mistake. We've now made massive investments to ensure this never happens again."

B. Cautious Argumentation

If a full acknowledgment isn't possible, explain what went wrong without undermining your responsibility:

- **Time pressure:** "We made decisions under extreme pressure, which led to mistakes."
- **Inexperience:** "We lacked experience in this type of situation."
- **Negligence:** "This was an oversight we shouldn't have made."

3. Crash – Keep Your Head Cool and Act with Structure

When the crisis involves personal attacks or serious mistakes, it can feel overwhelming. The **Then–Now–Since** model helps you maintain focus and navigate even in high-pressure situations.

- **Then:** What happened? What did the situation look like before?
- **Now:** What are we doing right now? What actions have we taken?
- **Since:** What is the next step? How do we prevent this from happening again?

SAS Handles the Ash Cloud of 2010

When the Eyjafjallajökull volcano in Iceland caused ash clouds that paralyzed air traffic across Europe, SAS found itself in the eye of the storm. Tens of thousands of travelers were stranded, planes were grounded, and criticism poured in.

SAS chose a clear communication strategy:

- **Then:** "The ash cloud has caused us to cancel all flights for safety reasons."
- **Now:** "We are focusing on helping travelers find alternatives and offering hotel and meal vouchers."
- **Since:** "We are developing a new crisis program to handle future disasters more quickly."

Despite the crisis, SAS earned respect for its clear, empathetic, and decisive actions.

Summary: The Core of Crisis Management

Crisis management is about acting quickly but thoughtfully. By creating clarity, stopping bleeding, and handling shock, you can not only manage the situation – but also use it to build trust and strengthen the organization.

Value-based leadership requires the courage to acknowledge mistakes, the strength to focus on solutions, and the empathy to consider both the team's and the customer's needs. In every crisis lies an opportunity to make a difference – if you dare to take it.

Crisis Management's Internal Communication

Balance. Calm. Patience. Trust.

When the storm is raging, the leader must become a lighthouse – steady, visible, and always aimed at the solution. In times of uncertainty, internal communication is not just important – it is crucial. Let clarity and forward-looking actions be the compass, while concrete activities become the rudder that steers the organization in the right direction.

And remember: Silence is not golden in a crisis. It's lead. Uncertainty fills the silence faster than you can say "We've got control."

Main statement – Let the Facts Speak (Without Frills)

Before any solutions are mentioned, lay the facts on the table. Turn "We think that ..." into "We know that ...". Facts are like a polished mirror – they reflect the situation without beautifying it.

- **The World Around Us:** Inflation, interest rates, or some new "buzzword" everyone's talking about? Provide a realistic picture of how this affects you.

- **Economy:** Is it time to tighten the belt or loosen the strings?
- **Product Portfolio:** Polish what shines and dare to consider dumping what's rusting.
- **Competence:** Is the team equipped for the challenge, or is reinforcement needed?

Let's not pretend we always know everything. Internal meetings lacking facts are like a blind leading another blind – you might be moving, but not in the right direction.

Sub statement – Shine the Light on the Present

Now, it's time to zoom in. What are we doing today? What are we prioritizing to move forward? No one wants to hear about future dreams if no action is taken today.

- **Focus on Solutions:** Which projects show that we're not standing still? An organization that moves forward gives hope.
- **The Trap of Passivity:** Every time we hit the brakes (layoffs, closures), we not only lose speed – we lose energy.

Virgin Trains faced a driverless crisis, literally. By communicating daily and focusing on what they were doing to resolve the situation (not just why it happened), they showed that movement – even in a crisis – creates direction.

Conclusion – Inspire Action

Set a clear direction with simple scenarios everyone can relate to. People don't need several shades of gray, they need clear choices:

1. **Cut down or wind down:** Prepare the world and the team if this becomes necessary.

2. **Maintain status quo:** If maintaining the current state is the goal, communicate why.
3. **Expand and grow:** Dare to aim high, but show how it will be done.

When SAS handled the pandemic crisis, they could have just said: "We don't know where the flight will land, but we know it's still taking off." Instead, they chose clear scenarios and maintained the trust of their staff.

Internal Communication in Practice

"No one expects perfection – but everyone expects honesty." Provide your employees with information before they read it in the newspaper. If you don't lead the story, someone else will.

Example: SAS during the pandemic. Through daily updates and the CEO's direct communication, they showed that transparency doesn't just manage the crisis, it strengthens the bonds.

Chapter 7.

Mental strategies and decision making

Making decisions is shaping the future.

Every decision we make, from the morning coffee to the last action of the day, builds our path forward. Decision-making is not just an art – it is a power that can lift us from uncertainty to clarity, from passivity to success. Here are some powerful strategies, stories, and tools to master the art of making decisions, even when the pressure is at its highest.

The Story of the Chinese Farmer

Once upon a time, a Chinese farmer lived with his son on a small farm. One day, their only horse ran away, and the neighbors lamented their bad luck. The farmer calmly smiled and responded:

"Good luck – bad luck, who knows?"

A few days later, the horse returned, and with it came five wild horses. "What great luck you have!" exclaimed the neighbors. The farmer shrugged and said:

"Good luck – bad luck, who knows?"

Shortly thereafter, the farmer's son broke his leg while trying to tame one of the horses. The neighbors sighed deeply: "How terrible!" But the farmer responded:

"Good luck – bad luck, who knows?"

A week later, the army came to recruit young men for war, but the farmer's son was allowed to stay home since he was injured. The neighbors congratulated him: "What great luck!" And the farmer responded, as always:

"Good luck – bad luck, who knows?"

Lesson:

This story teaches us that it's not what happens that defines us – it's how we handle it. Life is a constant balancing act between the expected and the unexpected, and our strength lies in maintaining calm, regardless of what happens.

Satya Nadella and Microsoft's Transformation

When Satya Nadella took over as CEO of Microsoft in 2014, the company was at a crossroads. It was stuck in old success models and had lost market share and reputation to competitors like Apple and Google. Internal conflicts and prestige projects had hindered development for years. Many wondered if Microsoft could even survive as a leading tech company.

Nadella realized that saving the company required bold decisions and a clear new direction. He did something radical: instead of clinging to Microsoft's traditional strengths (like Windows and Office), he focused relentlessly on cloud services, AI, and collaboration. He discontinued old projects that no longer created value and redirected all resources to future technology.

One of his most controversial decisions was to launch Microsoft Teams as a direct competitor to Slack, even though many internally were skeptical. But Nadella saw the potential and held firm to his vision. Today, Microsoft Teams is one of the most successful collaboration platforms, and the Azure cloud service is a leading global player.

Result?

Under Nadella's leadership, Microsoft has transformed from a stagnating company to an innovation giant. The company is now one of the world's most highly valued companies, with a culture that promotes collaboration, innovation, and learning.

What Can We Learn?

- Radical decisions require strong belief in the vision, even when others doubt.
- Sometimes, leaving old successes behind is necessary to create an even greater future.
- The culture in an organization is crucial – when people feel engaged and included, they can achieve great things.

The Art of Decision-Making – From Choice to Success

We live in a time of endless choices. According to research, we make between 2,000 and 10,000 decisions a day – from "What should I wear?" to "How should I navigate my career?" But here's the problem: Many of us get stuck in indecision, afraid of making the wrong choice. And what happens then? We do nothing at all.

But here's the secret: Decisions don't have to be perfect – and they don't need to be. Success is about daring to choose, even when the way forward is uncertain. Because if you don't move forward, you stay still. And if you stay still, you miss the chance to grow.

Three Mental Strategies for Better Decision-Making

1. **Prioritize like a laser beam, not a lightbulb**
   Focus on what truly matters right now. Identify your strengths and align them with your goal. As Sun Tzu said 3,500 years ago:
   "Strategy without tactics is the slowest route to victory. Tactics without strategy are the noise before defeat."
2. **Let the whole picture lead**
   Think long-term. Each decision should bring you closer to your overarching goals, not just solve today's problems. Success is like a puzzle – each piece must fit into the whole.
3. **Be flexible, but stay the course**

Life is not a straight path. Learn to adapt to changes, but never let short-term challenges make you forget your long-term goals. Just like in chess: You might lose a piece, but the game continues.

Three Practical Tips for Better Decision-Making

1. **Make decisions quickly – indecision is a thief of time and energy**
   Don't let the fear of making the wrong choice stop you from choosing at all. A decision is always better than no decision.
2. **Make a simple pros and cons list**
   Write down the advantages and disadvantages. When you see the options clearly, it becomes easier to identify the right path.
3. **Sleep on it**
   Give your brain time to process. A good night's sleep can give you perspective and clarity that's not available in the moment.

> *"Success is not final, failure is not fatal – it is the courage to continue that count." – Winston Churchill*

Summary: The Courage to Choose, the Strength to Hold On

Decision-making is about courage. The courage to choose a direction, the courage to hold on to it, and the courage to adjust if needed. When you learn to prioritize strategy over tactics and long-term goals over short-term ones, you're not just building success – you're building something that lasts a lifetime.

So the next time you face a decision, big or small, ask yourself these questions:
- Is this in line with my long-term goals?
- Am I making a decision based on fear – or on opportunities?
- What can I learn, regardless of the outcome?

And most importantly: Dare to choose. Every decision is a step forward, and it is in movement that we create the future.

Conclusion for Part 3: Leading the Organization – Your Journey Starts Here

Leading an organization is like being the captain of a ship navigating through a constantly changing world. It's not just about following a map – it's about redrawing it when the wind shifts and the waves strike. It takes courage to make tough decisions, humility to learn from every situation, and a passion to drive forward, regardless of the challenges.

In this section, we have explored the foundations of successful organizational leadership:

- How to build strategic cornerstones that provide direction and stability.
- How to embrace agility and learn to dance with change.
- How to dare to choose growth and turn obstacles into opportunities.
- How to balance the opposites of leadership – delegating with clarity and making uncompromising decisions when required.
- And how, with the RAK model, you can create clarity in goals, activities, and competence to achieve long-term results.

But leadership is more than strategies and models. It is a journey that starts in your heart and extends throughout the organization. It's a value-based commitment – to be the one who dares to see further, inspire bigger, and create a culture where each person feels part of something greater.

As you close this part and look ahead, ask yourself:

- What is the most important thing I want to leave behind as a leader?
- How can I inspire my team to reach its full potential?
- What impact do I want our organization to make in the world?

As Lao Tzu aptly expressed: "When a good leader does his work, the people feel like they did it themselves."

You have the power to be that leader. The one who not only drives the organization forward but also creates meaning, hope, and inspiration along the way. Your journey begins here – and the future awaits to be shaped by your courage and vision.

So **take the helm. Set the course**. And sail toward the horizon with courage, clarity, and a strong belief in what you and your organization can achieve.

Reflection Questions – Take Your Leadership to the Next Level

1. **What strategic foundation do I need to strengthen?**
    -   Is there a clear direction for my organization, and how do I ensure that everyone on the team understands and shares that vision?

2. **How can I become more agile as a leader?**
    -   How quickly do I and my organization adapt to changes, and what concrete steps can I take to enhance our flexibility?

3. **What obstacles can I turn into opportunities?**
    -   Identify a current problem in your organization. How can you use limitations as a creative force to find innovative solutions?

4. **How do I balance long-term growth with daily challenges?**
    -   In what areas can I improve at delegating and creating clearer priorities to both handle the immediate and build for the future?

5. **How do I apply the RAK model in my organization?**
    -   What is the most important result I want to achieve in the next three months? What activities and competencies are required to get us there?

Final words: Lead for real – or step aside

Leadership is about one thing: Action. It is always action that separates people. Everyone can talk. Everyone can give nice talks about values, visions, and team spirit. But who does it? Who steps into the ring and takes responsibility? Who is left standing when the wind blows? There you have the difference between talk and leadership.

Do you want to be the one who sits on the bench and analyzes? Or do you want to be the one who steps in and controls the game? It's your choice. But remember: **nothing happens until someone does something.**

This book has given you the tools. How to lead yourself, how to lift others, how to build a company that actually matters. But no book in the world can lead you to that. You have to do it yourself. It's simple: Either you act or you don't.

Want to create results? Then it's time to **release the handbrake**. Stand in front of the mirror and ask yourself: Are you ready to lead for real? Because if you're not, then it's time to step aside and let someone else take over.

But if you're ready? Summon up the courage and step into the arena on the next level, life is short and unpredictable.

Good luck!